THE COLLECTED WORKS OF WILLIAM FAULKNER

✶

REQUIEM FOR A NUN

D1231673

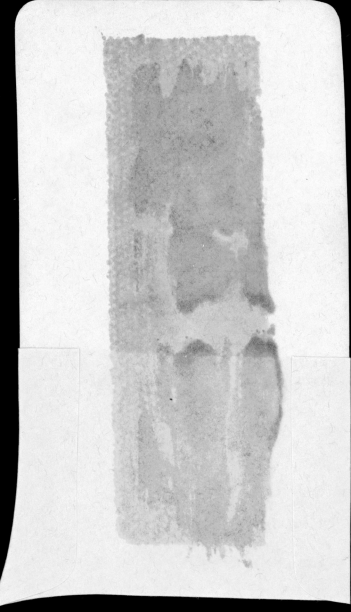

REQUIEM FOR A NUN

William Faulkner

1965

CHATTO & WINDUS

LONDON

PUBLISHED BY
Chatto and Windus Ltd
42 William IV Street
London W.C.2

First published in Great Britain
1953

*Printed in Great Britain by
Lowe and Brydone (Printers) Limited
London*

CONTENTS

REQUIEM FOR A NUN

ACT ONE

THE COURTHOUSE (A Name for the City)

The courthouse is less old than the town, which began
somewhere under the turn of the century as a Chickasaw
Agency trading-post and so continued for almost thirty
years before it discovered, not that it lacked a depository
for its records and certainly not that it needed one, but
that only by creating or anyway decreeing one, could it
cope with a situation which otherwise was going to cost
somebody money;

The settlement had the records; even the simple dispossession of Indians begot in time a minuscule of archive,
let alone the normal litter of man's ramshackle confederation against environment—that time and that wilderness
—in this case, a meagre, fading, dog-eared, uncorrelated,
at times illiterate sheaf of land grants and patents and
transfers and deeds, and tax- and militia-rolls, and bills of
sale for slaves, and counting-house lists of spurious cur-
rency and exchange rates, and liens and mortgages, and
listed rewards for escaped or stolen Negroes and other
livestock, and diary-like annotations of births and mar-
riages and deaths and public hangings and land-auctions,
accumulating slowly for those three decades in a sort of
iron pirate's chest in the back room of the post-office-
trading-post-store, until that day thirty years later when,
because of a jailbreak compounded by an ancient monster
iron padlock transported a thousand miles by horseback
from Carolina, the box was removed to a small new
lean-to room like a wood- or tool-shed built two days

ago against one outside wall of the morticed-log mud-chinked shake-down jail; and thus was born the Yoknapatawpha County courthouse: by simple fortuity, not only less old than even the jail, but come into existence at all by chance and accident: the box containing the documents not moved from any place, but simply to one; removed from the trading-post back room not for any reason inherent in either the back room or the box, but on the contrary: which—the box—was not only in nobody's way in the back room, it was even missed when gone since it had served as another seat or stool among the powder- and whiskey-kegs and firkins of salt and lard about the stove on winter nights; and was moved at all for the simple reason that suddenly the settlement (overnight it would become a town without having been a village; one day in about a hundred years it would wake frantically from its communal slumber into a rash of Rotary and Lion Clubs and Chambers of Commerce and City Beautifuls: a furious beating of hollow drums toward nowhere, but merely to sound louder than the next little human clotting to its north or south or east or west, dubbing itself city as Napoleon dubbed himself emperor and defending the expedient by padding its census rolls —a fever, a delirium in which it would confound forever seething with motion and motion with progress. But that was a hundred years away yet; now it was frontier, the men and women pioneers, tough, simple, and durable, seeking money or adventure or freedom or simple escape, and not too particular how they did it.) discovered itself faced not so much with a problem which had to be solved, as a Damocles sword of dilemma from which it had to save itself;

Even the jailbreak was fortuity: a gang—three or four—
of Natchez Trace bandits (twenty-five years later legend
would begin to affirm, and a hundred years later would
still be at it, that two of the bandits were the Harpes
themselves, Big Harpe anyway, since the circumstances,
the method of the breakout left behind like a smell, an
odour, a kind of gargantuan and bizarre playfulness at
once humorous and terrifying, as if the settlement had
fallen, blundered, into the notice or range of an idle and
whimsical giant. Which—that they were the Harpes—was
impossible, since the Harpes and even the last of Mason's
ruffians were dead or scattered by this time, and the rob-
bers would have had to belong to John Murrel's organisa-
tion—if they needed to belong to any at all other than the
simple fraternity of rapine.) captured by chance by an in-
cidental band of civilian more-or-less militia and brought
in to the Jefferson jail because it was the nearest one, the
militia band being part of a general muster at Jefferson
two days before for a Fourth-of-July barbecue, which by
the second day had been refined by hardy elimination into
one drunken brawling which rendered even the hardiest
survivors vulnerable enough to be ejected from the settlement by the civilian residents, the band which was to
make the capture having been carried, still comatose, in
one of the evicting wagons to a swamp four miles from
Jefferson known as Hurricane Bottoms, where they made
camp to regain their strength or at least their legs, and
where that night the four—or three—bandits, on the way
across country to their hide-out from their last exploit on
the Trace, stumbled onto the campfire. And here report
divided; some said that the sergeant in command of the
militia recognised one of the bandits as a deserter from his

corps, others said that one of the bandits recognised in the sergeant a former follower of his, the bandit's, trade. Anyway, on the fourth morning all of them, captors and prisoners, returned to Jefferson in a group, some said in confederation now seeking more drink, others said that the captors brought their prizes back to the settlement in revenge for having been evicted from it. Because these were frontier, pioneer times, when personal liberty and freedom were almost a physical condition like fire or flood, and no community was going to interfere with anyone's morals as long as the amoralist practised somewhere else, and so Jefferson, being neither on the Trace nor the River but lying about midway between, naturally wanted no part of the underworld of either;

But they had some of it now, taken as it were by surprise, unawares, without warning to prepare and fend off. They put the bandits into the log-and-mud-chinking jail, which until now had had no lock at all since its clients so far had been amateurs—local brawlers and drunkards and runaway slaves—for whom a single heavy wooden beam in slots across the outside of the door like on a corncrib, had sufficed. But they had now what might be four—three—Dillingers or Jesse Jameses of the time, with rewards on their heads. So they locked the jail; they bored an auger hole through the door and another through the jamb and passed a length of heavy chain through the holes and sent a messenger on the run across to the post-office-store to fetch the ancient Carolina lock from the last Nashville mail-pouch—the iron monster weighing almost fifteen pounds, with a key almost as long as a bayonet, not just the only lock in that part of the country, but the oldest

lock in that cranny of the United States, brought there
by one of the three men who were what was to be Yoknapatawpha County's coeval pioneers and settlers, leaving
in it the three oldest names—Alexander Holston, who
came as half groom and half bodyguard to Doctor Samuel
Habersham, and half nurse and half tutor to the doctor's
eight-year-old motherless son, the three of them riding
horseback across Tennessee from the Cumberland Gap
along with Louis Grenier, the Huguenot younger son
who brought the first slaves into the country and was
granted the first big land patent and so became the first
cotton planter; while Doctor Habersham, with his worn
black bag of pills and knives and his brawny taciturn
bodyguard and his half orphan child, became the settlement itself (for a time, before it was named, the settlement was known as Doctor Habersham's, then Habersham's, then simply Habersham ; a hundred years later,
during a schism between two ladies' clubs over the
naming of the streets in order to get free mail delivery, a
movement was started, first, to change the name back to
Habersham; then, failing that, to divide the town in two
and call one half of it Habersham after the old pioneer
doctor and founder)—friend of old Issetibbeha, the Chickasaw chief (the motherless Habersham boy, now a man
of twenty-five, married one of Issetibbeha's grand-
daughters and in the thirties emigrated to Oklahoma with
his wife's dispossessed people), first unofficial, then official
Chickasaw agent until he resigned in a letter of furious
denunciation addressed to the President of the United
States himself; and—his charge and pupil a man now—
Alexander Holston became the settlement's first publi-
can, establishing the tavern still known as the Holston

House, the original log walls and puncheon floors and hand-morticed joints of which are still buried somewhere beneath the modern pressed glass and brick veneer and neon tubes. The lock was his;

Fifteen pounds of useless iron lugged a thousand miles through a desert of precipice and swamp, of flood and drouth and wild beasts and wild Indians and wilder white men, displacing that fifteen pounds better given to food or seed to plant food or even powder to defend with, to become a fixture, a kind of landmark, in the bar of a wilderness ordinary, locking and securing nothing, because there was nothing behind the heavy bars and shutters needing further locking and securing; not even a paper weight because the only papers in the Holston House were the twisted spills in an old powder horn above the mantel for lighting tobacco; always a little in the way, since it had constantly to be moved: from bar to shelf to mantel then back to bar again until they finally thought about putting it on the bi-monthly mail-pouch; familiar, known, presently the oldest unchanged thing in the settlement, older than the people since Issetibbeha and Doctor Habersham were dead, and Alexander Holston was an old man crippled with arthritis, and Louis Grenier had a settlement of his own on his vast plantation, half of which was not even in Yoknapatawpha County, and the settlement rarely saw him; older than the town, since there were new names in it now even when the old blood ran in them—Sartoris and Stevens, Compson and McCaslin and Sutpen and Coldfield—and you no longer shot a bear or deer or wild turkey simply by standing for a while in your kitchen door, not to mention the pouch of mail—·

letters and even newspapers—which came from Nashville
every two weeks by a special rider who did nothing else
and was paid a salary for it by the Federal Government;
and that was the second phase of the monster Carolina
lock's transubstantiation into the Yoknapatawpha County
courthouse;

The pouch didn't always reach the settlement every two
weeks, nor even always every month. But sooner or later
it did, and everybody knew it would, because it—the
cowhide saddlebag not even large enough to hold a full
change of clothing, containing three or four letters and
half that many badly-printed one- and two-sheet newspapers already three or four months out of date and
usually half and sometimes wholly misinformed or incor-
rect to begin with—was the United States, the power and
the will to liberty, owning liegence to no man, bringing
even into that still almost pathless wilderness the thin
peremptory voice of the nation which had wrenched its
freedom from one of the most powerful peoples on earth
and then again within the same lifespan successfully
defended it; so peremptory and audible that the man who
carried the pouch on the galloping horse didn't even carry
any arms except a tin horn, traversing month after month,
blatantly, flagrantly, almost contemptuously, a region
where for no more than the boots on his feet, men would
murder a traveller and gut him like a bear or deer or fish
and fill the cavity with rocks and sink the evidence in the
nearest water; not even deigning to pass quietly where
other men, even though armed and in parties, tried to
move secretly or at least without uproar, but instead
announcing his solitary advent as far ahead of himself as

the ring of the horn would carry. So it was not long before
Alexander Holston's lock had moved to the mail-pouch.
Not that the pouch needed one, having come already the
three hundred miles from Nashville without a lock. (It
had been projected at first that the lock remain on the
pouch constantly. That is, not just while the pouch was
in the settlement, but while it was on the horse between
Nashville and the settlement too. The rider refused, suc-
cinctly, in three words, one of which was printable. His
reason was the lock's weight. They pointed out to him
that this would not hold water, since not only—the rider
was a frail irascible little man weighing less than a hundred
pounds—would the fifteen pounds of lock even then fail
to bring his weight up to that of a normal adult male, the
added weight of the lock would merely match that of
the pistols which his employer, the United States Government, believed he carried and even paid him for having
done so, the rider's reply to this being succinct too though
not so glib: that the lock weighed fifteen pounds either
at the back door of the store in the settlement, or at that
of the post-office in Nashville. But since Nashville and the
settlement were three hundred miles apart, by the time
the horse had carried it from one to the other, the lock
weighed fifteen pounds to the mile times three hundred
miles, or forty-five hundred pounds. Which was manifest
nonsense, a physical impossibility either in lock or horse.
Yet indubitably fifteen pounds times three hundred miles
was forty-five hundred something, either pounds or
miles—especially as while they were still trying to un-
ravel it, the rider repeated his first three succinct—two
unprintable—words.) So less than ever would the pouch
need a lock in the back room of the trading-post, sur-

rounded and enclosed once more by civilisation, where
its very intactness, its presence to receive a lock, proved
its lack of that need during the three hundred miles of
rapine-haunted Trace; needing a lock as little as it was
equipped to receive one, since it had been necessary to
slit the leather with a knife just under each jaw of the
opening and insert the lock's iron mandible through the
two slits and clash it home, so that any other hand with a
similar knife could have cut the whole lock from the
pouch as easily as it had been clasped onto it. So the old
lock was not even a symbol of security; it was a gesture
of salutation, of free men to free men, of civilisation to
civilisation across not just the three hundred miles of
wilderness to Nashville, but the fifteen hundred to Washington: of respect without servility, allegiance without
abasement to the government which they had helped to
found and had accepted with pride but still as free men,
still free to withdraw from it at any moment when the
two of them found themselves no longer compatible, the
old lock meeting the pouch each time on its arrival, to
clasp it in iron and inviolable symbolism, while old Alec
Holston, childless bachelor, grew a little older and greyer,
a little more arthritic in flesh and temper too, a little
stiffer and more rigid in bone and pride too, since the
lock was still his, he had merely lent it, and so in a sense
he was the grandfather in the settlement of the inviol-
ability not just of government mail, but of a free government of free men too, so long as the government remembered to let men live free, not under it but beside it;

That was the lock; they put it on the jail. They did it
quickly, not even waiting until a messenger could have

got back from the Holston House with old Alec's permission to remove it from the mail-pouch or use it for the new purpose. Not that he would have objected on principle nor refused his permission except by simple instinct; that is, he would probably have been the first to suggest the lock if he had known in time or thought of it first, but he would have refused at once if he thought the thing was contemplated without consulting him. Which everybody in the settlement knew, though this was not at all why they didn't wait for the messenger. In fact, no messenger had ever been sent to old Alec; they didn't have time to send one, let alone wait until he got back; they didn't want the lock to keep the bandits in, since (as was later proved) the old lock would have been no more obstacle for the bandits to pass than the customary wooden bar; they didn't need the lock to protect the settlement from the bandits, but to protect the bandits from the settlement. Because the prisoners had barely reached the settlement when it developed that there was a faction bent on lynching them at once, out of hand, without preliminary—a small but determined gang which tried to wrest the prisoners from their captors while the militia was still trying to find someone to surrender them to, and would have succeeded except for a man named Compson, who had come to the settlement a few years ago with a race-horse, which he swapped to Ikkemotubbe, Issetibbeha's successor in the chiefship, for a square mile of what was to be the most valuable land in the future town of Jefferson, who, legend said, drew a pistol and held the ravishers at bay until the bandits could be got into the jail and the auger holes bored and someone sent to fetch old Alec Holston's lock. Because there were

indeed new names and faces too in the settlement now—
faces so new as to have (to the older residents) no discernible antecedents other than mammalinity, nor past
other than the simple years which had scored them; and
names so new as to have no discernible (nor discoverable
either) antecedents or past at all, as though they had been
invented yesterday, report dividing again: to the effect
that there were more people in the settlement that day
than the militia sergeant whom one or all of the bandits
might recognise;

So Compson locked the jail, and a courier with the two
best horses in the settlement—one to ride and one to lead
—cut through the woods to the Trace to ride the hun-
dred-odd miles to Natchez with news of the capture and
authority to dicker for the reward; and that evening in
the Holston House kitchen was held the settlement's first
municipal meeting, prototype not only of the town council after the settlement would be a town, but of the
Chamber of Commerce when it would begin to proclaim
itself a city, with Compson presiding, not old Alec, who
was quite old now, grim, taciturn, sitting even on a hot
July night before a smouldering log in his vast chimney,
his back even turned to the table (he was not interested in
the deliberation; the prisoners were his already since his
lock held them; whatever the conference decided would
have to be submitted to him for ratification anyway
before anyone could touch his lock to open it) around
which the progenitors of the Jefferson city fathers sat in
what was almost a council of war, not only discussing the
collecting of the reward, but the keeping and defending
it. Because there were two factions of opposition now:

not only the lynching party, but the militia band too, who
now claimed that as prizes the prisoners still belonged to
their original captors; that they—the militia—had merely
surrendered the prisoners' custody but had relinquished
nothing of any reward: on the prospect of which, the
militia band had got more whiskey from the trading-post
store and had built a tremendous bonfire in front of the
jail, around which they and the lynching party had now
confederated in a wassail or conference of their own. Or
so they thought. Because the truth was that Compson, in
the name of a crisis in the public peace and welfare, had
made a formal demand on the professional bag of Doctor
Peabody, old Doctor Habersham's successor, and the three
of them—Compson, Peabody, and the post trader (his
name was Ratcliffe; a hundred years later it would still
exist in the county, but by that time it had passed through
two inheritors who had dispensed with the eye in the
transmission of words, using only the ear, so that by the
time the fourth one had been compelled by simple necessity to learn to write it again, it had lost the 'c' and the
final 'fe' too) added the laudanum to the keg of whiskey
and sent it as a gift from the settlement to the astonished
militia sergeant, and returned to the Holston House
kitchen to wait until the last of the uproar died; then the
law-and-order party made a rapid sortie and gathered up
all the comatose opposition, lynchers and captors too, and
dumped them all into the jail with the prisoners and
locked the door again and went home to bed—until the
next morning, when the first arrivals were met by a scene
resembling an outdoor stage setting: which was how the
legend of the mad Harpes started: a thing not just fan-
tastical but incomprehensible, not just whimsical but a

little terrifying (though at least it was bloodless, which
would have contented neither Harpe): not just the lock
gone from the door nor even just the door gone from the
jail, but the entire wall gone, the mud-chinked axe-
morticed logs unjointed neatly and quietly in the darkness
and stacked as neatly to one side, leaving the jail open to
the world like a stage on which the late insurgents still lay
sprawled and various in deathlike slumber, the whole
settlement gathered now to watch Compson trying to
kick at least one of them awake, until one of the Holston
slaves—the cook's husband, the waiter-groom-hostler—
ran into the crowd shouting, 'Whar de lock, whar de
lock, ole Boss say whar de lock.'

It was gone (as were three horses belonging to three of
the lynching faction). They couldn't even find the heavy
door and the chain, and at first they were almost betrayed
into believing that the bandits had had to take the door
in order to steal the chain and lock, catching themselves
back from the very brink of this wanton accusation of
rationality. But the lock was gone; nor did it take the
settlement long to realise that it was not the escaped
bandits and the aborted reward, but the lock, and not a
simple situation which faced them, but a problem which
threatened, the slave departing back to the Holston House
at a dead run and then reappearing at the dead run almost
before the door, the walls, had had time to hide him,
engulf and then eject him again, darting through the
crowd and up to Compson himself now, saying, 'Ole
Boss say fetch de lock'—not send the lock, but bring the
lock. So Compson and his lieutenants (and this was where
the mail rider began to appear, or rather, to emerge—

the fragile wisp of a man ageless, hairless and toothless,
who looked too frail even to approach a horse, let alone
ride one six hundred miles every two weeks, yet who did
to, and not only that but had wind enough left not only
so announce and precede but even follow his passing with
the jeering musical triumph of the horn:—a contempt for
possible—probable—despoilers matched only by that for
the official dross of which he might be despoiled, and
which agreed to remain in civilised bounds only so long
as the despoilers had the taste to refrain)—repaired to the
kitchen where old Alec still sat before his smouldering
log, his back still to the room, and still not turning it this
time either. And that was all. He ordered the immediate
return of his lock. It was not even an ultimatum, it was a
simple instruction, a decree, impersonal, the mail rider
now well into the fringe of the group, saying nothing and
missing nothing, like a weightless desiccated or fossil bird,
not a vulture of course nor even quite a hawk, but say a
pterodactyl chick arrested just out of the egg ten glaciers
ago and so old in simple infancy as to be the worn and
weary ancestor of all subsequent life. They pointed out to
old Alec that the only reason the lock could be missing
was that the bandits had not had time or been able to cut
it out of the door and that even three fleeing madmen on
stolen horses would not carry a six-foot oak door very
far, and that a party of Ikkemotubbe's young men were
even now trailing the horses westward toward the River
and that without doubt the lock would be found at any
moment, probably under the first bush at the edge of the
settlement: knowing better, knowing that there was no
limit to the fantastic and the terrifying and the bizarre, of
which the men were capable who already, just to escape

from a log jail, had quietly removed one entire wall and stacked it in neat piecemeal at the roadside, and that they nor old Alec neither would ever see his lock again;

Nor did they; the rest of that afternoon and all the next day too, while old Alec still smoked his pipe in front of his smouldering log, the settlement's sheepish and raging elders hunted for it, with (by now: the next afternoon) Ikkemotubbe's Chickasaws helping too, or anyway present, watching: the wild men, the wilderness's tameless evictant children looking only the more wild and homeless for the white man's denim and butternut and felt and straw which they wore, standing or squatting or following, grave, attentive and interested, while the white men sweated and cursed among the bordering thickets of their punily-clawed foothold; and always the rider, Pettigrew, ubiquitous, everywhere, not helping search himself and never in anyone's way, but always present, inscrutable, saturnine, missing nothing: until at last toward sundown Compson crashed savagely out of the last bramble-brake and flung the sweat from his face with a full-armed sweep sufficient to repudiate a throne, and said,

'All right, god damn it, we'll pay him for it.' Because they had already considered that last gambit; they had already realised its seriousness from the very fact that Peabody had tried to make a joke about it which everyone knew that even Peabody did not think humorous:

'Yes—and quick too, before he has time to advise with Pettigrew and price it by the pound.'

'By the pound?' Compson said.

'Pettigrew just weighed it by the three hundred

miles from Nashville. Old Alec might start from Carolina. That's fifteen thousand pounds.'

'Oh,' Compson said. So he blew in his men by
means of a foxhorn which one of the Indians wore on a
thong around his neck, though even then they paused for
one last quick conference; again it was Peabody who
stopped them.

'Who'll pay for it?' he said. 'It would be just like
him to want a dollar a pound for it, even if by Pettigrew's
scale he had found it in the ashes of his fireplace.' They—
Compson anyway—had probably already thought of
that; that, as much as Pettigrew's presence, was probably
why he was trying to rush them into old Alec's presence
with the offer so quickly that none would have the face
to renegue on a pro-rata share. But Peabody had torn it
now. Compson looked about at them, sweating, grimly
enraged.

'That means Peabody will probably pay one dollar,' he said. 'Who pays the other fourteen? Me?' Then
Ratcliffe, the trader, the store's proprietor, solved it—a
solution so simple, so limitless in retroact, that they didn't
even wonder why nobody had thought of it before;
which not only solved the problem but abolished it; and
not just that one, but all problems, from now on into
perpetuity, opening to their vision like the rending of a
veil, like a glorious prophecy, the vast splendid limitless
panorama of America: that land of boundless opportunity, that bourne, created not by nor of the people, but
for the people, as was the heavenly manna of old, with
no return demand on man save the chewing and swallow-
ing since out of its own matchless Allgood it would create
produce train support and perpetuate a race of labourers

dedicated to the single purpose of picking the manna up and putting it into his lax hand or even between his jaws —illimitable, vast, without beginning or end, not even a trade or a craft but a beneficence as are sunlight and rain and air, inalienable and immutable.

'Put it on the Book,' Ratcliffe said—the Book: not a ledger, but *the* ledger, since it was probably the only thing of its kind between Nashville and Natchez, unless there might happen to be a similar one a few miles south at the first Choctaw agency at Yalo Busha—a ruled, paper-backed copybook such as might have come out of a schoolroom, in which accrued, with the United States as debtor, in Mohataha's name (the Chickasaw matriarch, Ikkemotubbe's mother and old Issetibbeha's sister, who —she could write her name, or anyway make something with a pen or pencil which was agreed to be, or at least accepted to be, a valid signature—signed all the conveyances as her son's kingdom passed to the white people, regularising it in law anyway) the crawling tedious list of calico and gunpowder, whiskey and salt and snuff and denim pants and osseous candy drawn from Ratcliffe's shelves by her descendants and subjects and Negro slaves. That was all the settlement had to do: add the lock to the list, the account. It wouldn't even matter at what price they entered it. They could have priced it on Pettigrew's scale of fifteen pounds times the distance not just to Carolina but to Washington itself, and nobody would ever notice it probably; they could have charged the United States with seventeen thousand five hundred dollars' worth of the fossilised and indestructible candy, and none would ever read the entry. So it was solved, done, finished, ended. They didn't even have to discuss it.

They didn't even think about it any more, unless perhaps here and there to marvel (a little speculatively probably) at their own moderation, since they wanted nothing—least of all, to escape any just blame—but a fair and decent adjustment of the lock. They went back to where old Alec still sat with his pipe in front of his dim hearth. Only they had overestimated him; he didn't want any money at all, he wanted his lock. Whereupon what little remained of Compson's patience went too.

'Your lock's gone,' he told old Alec harshly. 'You'll take fifteen dollars for it,' he said, his voice already fading, because even that rage could recognise impasse when it saw it. Nevertheless, the rage, the impotence, the sweating, the *too much*—whatever it was—forced the voice on for one word more: 'Or——' before it stopped for good and allowed Peabody to fill the gap:

'Or else?' Peabody said, and not to old Alec, but to Compson. 'Or else what?' Then Ratcliffe saved that too.

'Wait,' he said. 'Uncle Alec's going to take fifty dollars for his lock. A guarantee of fifty dollars. He'll give us the name of the blacksmith back in Cal'lina that made it for him, and we'll send back there and have a new one made. Going and coming and all'll cost about fifty dollars. We'll give Uncle Alec the fifty dollars to hold as a guarantee. Then when the new lock comes, he'll give us back the money. All right, Uncle Alec?' And that could have been all of it. It probably would have been, except for Pettigrew. It was not that they had forgotten him, nor even assimilated him. They had simply sealed—healed him off (so they thought)—him into their civic crisis as the desperate and defenceless oyster immobilises its atom of inevictable grit. Nobody had seen him move yet he now stood in the centre of them where Compson and Ratcliffe and Peabody faced old Alec in the chair. You might have said that he had oozed there, except for that adamantine quality which might (in emergency) become invisible but never insubstantial and never in this world fluid; he spoke in a voice bland, reasonable and impersonal, then stood there being looked at, frail and child-sized, impermeable as diamond and manifest with portent, bringing into that backwoods room a thousand miles deep in pathless wilderness, the whole vast incalculable weight of federality, not just representing the government nor even himself just the government; for that moment at least, he was the United States.

'Uncle Alec hasn't lost any lock,' he said. 'That was Uncle Sam.'

After a moment someone said, 'What?'

'That's right,' Pettigrew said. 'Whoever put that lock of Holston's on that mail bag either made a voluntary gift to the United States, and the same law covers the United States Government that covers minor children; you can give something to them, but you can't take it back, or he or they done something else.'

They looked at him. Again after a while somebody said something; it was Ratcliffe. 'What else?' Ratcliffe said. Pettigrew answered, still bland, impersonal, heatless and glib: 'Committed a violation of act of Congress as especially made and provided for the defacement of government property, penalty of five thousand dollars or not less than one year in a Federal jail or both. For whoever cut them two slits in the bag to put the lock in, act of Congress as especially made and provided for the injury

or destruction of government property, penalty of ten
thousand dollars or not less than five years in a Federal
jail or both.' He did not move even yet; he simply spoke
directly to old Alec: 'I reckon you're going to have
supper here same as usual sooner or later or more or less.'

'Wait,' Ratcliffe said. He turned to Compson. 'Is
that true?'

'What the hell difference does it make whether it's
true or not?' Compson said. 'What do you think he's
going to do as soon as he gets to Nashville?' He said
violently to Pettigrew: 'You were supposed to leave for
Nashville yesterday. What were you hanging around
here for?'

'Nothing to go to Nashville for,' Pettigrew said.
'You don't want any mail. You ain't got anything to lock
it up with.'

'So we ain't,' Ratcliffe said. 'So we'll let the United
States find the United States' lock.' This time Pettigrew
looked at no one. He wasn't even speaking to anyone,
any more than old Alec had been when he decreed the
return of his lock:

'Act of Congress as made and provided for the
unauthorised removal and or use or wilful or felonious
use or misuse or loss of government property, penalty the
value of the article plus five hundred to ten thousand
dollars or thirty days to twenty years in a Federal jail or
both. They may even make a new one when they read
where you have charged a post-office department lock to
the Bureau of Indian Affairs.' He moved; now he was
speaking to old Alec again: 'I'm going out to my horse.
When this meeting is over and you get back to cooking,
you can send your nigger for me.'

Then he was gone. After a while Ratcliffe said, 'What do you reckon he aims to get out of this? A reward?' But that was wrong; they all knew better than that.

'He's already getting what he wants,' Compson said, and cursed again. 'Confusion. Just damned confusion.' But that was wrong too; they all knew that too, though it was Peabody who said it:

'No. Not confusion. A man who will ride six hundred miles through this country every two weeks, with nothing for protection but a foxhorn, ain't really interested in confusion any more than he is in money.' So they didn't know yet what was in Pettigrew's mind. But they knew what he would do. That is, they knew that they did not know at all, either what he would do, or how, or when, and that there was nothing whatever that they could do about it until they discovered why. And they saw now that they had no possible means to discover that; they realised now that they had known him for three years now, during which, fragile and inviolable and undeviable and preceded for a mile or more by the strong sweet ringing of the horn, on his strong and tireless horse he would complete the bi-monthly trip from Nashville to the settlement and for the next three or four days would live among them, yet that they knew nothing whatever about him, and even now knew only that they dared not, simply dared not, take any chance, sitting for a while longer in the darkening room while old Alec still smoked, his back still squarely turned to them and their quandary too; then dispersing to their own cabins for the evening meal— with what appetite they could bring to it, since presently they had drifted back through the summer darkness when by ordinary they would have been already in bed, to the back room of Ratcliffe's store now, to sit again while Ratcliffe recapitulated in his mixture of bewilderment and alarm (and something else which they recognised was respect as they realised that he—Ratcliffe—was unshakably convinced that Pettigrew's aim was money; that Pettigrew had invented or evolved a scheme so richly rewarding that he—Ratcliffe—had not only been unable to forestall him and do it first, he—Radcliffe—couldn't even guess what it was after he had been given a hint) until Compson interrupted him.

'Hell,' Compson said. 'Everybody knows what's wrong with him. It's ethics. He's a damned moralist.'

'Ethics?' Peabody said. He sounded almost startled. He said quickly: 'That's bad. How can we corrupt an ethical man?'

'Who wants to corrupt him?' Compson said. 'All we want him to do is stay on that damned horse and blow whatever extra wind he's got into that damned horn.'

But Peabody was not even listening. He said, 'Ethics,' almost dreamily. He said, 'Wait.' They watched him. He said suddenly to Ratcliffe: 'I've heard it somewhere. If anybody here knows it, it'll be you. What's his name?'

'His name?' Ratcliffe said. 'Pettigrew's? Oh. His christian name.' Ratcliffe told him. 'Why?'

'Nothing,' Peabody said. 'I'm going home. Anybody else coming?' He spoke directly to nobody and said and would say no more, but that was enough: a straw perhaps, but at least a straw; enough anyway for the others to watch and say nothing either as Compson got up too and said to Ratcliffe:

'You coming?' and the three of them walked away together, beyond earshot then beyond sight too. Then Compson said, 'All right. What?'

'It may not work,' Peabody said. 'But you two will have to back me up. When I speak for the whole settlement, you and Ratcliffe will have to make it stick. Will you?'

Compson cursed. 'But at least tell us a little of what we're going to guarantee.' So Peabody told them some of it, and the next morning entered the stall in the Holston House stable where Pettigrew was grooming his ugly hammer-headed iron-muscled horse.

'We decided not to charge that lock to old Mohataha, after all,' Peabody said.

'That so?' Pettigrew said. 'Nobody in Washington would ever catch it. Certainly not the ones that can read.'

'We're going to pay for it ourselves,' Peabody said. 'In fact, we're going to do a little more. We've got to repair that jail wall anyhow; we've got to build one wall anyway. So by building three more, we will have another room. We got to build one anyway, so that don't count. So by building an extra three-wall room, we will have another four-wall house. That will be the courthouse.' Pettigrew had been hissing gently between his teeth at each stroke of the brush, like a professional Irish groom. Now he stopped, the brush and his hand arrested in midstroke, and turned his head a little.

'Courthouse?'

'We're going to have a town,' Peabody said. 'We already got a church—that's Whitfield's cabin. And we're going to build a school too soon as we get around to it.

But we're going to build the courthouse today; we've already got something to put in it to make it a courthouse: that iron box that's been in Ratcliffe's way in the store for the last ten years. Then we'll have a town. We've already even named her.'

Now Pettigrew stood up, very slowly. They looked at one another. After a moment Pettigrew said, 'So?'

'Ratcliffe says your name's Jefferson,' Peabody said.

'That's right,' Pettigrew said. 'Thomas Jefferson Pettigrew. I'm from old Ferginny.'

'Any kin?' Peabody said.

'No,' Pettigrew said. 'My ma named me for him, so I would have some of his luck.'

'Luck?' Peabody said.

Pettigrew didn't smile. 'That's right. She didn't mean luck. She never had any schooling. She didn't know the word she wanted to say.'

'Have you had it?' Peabody said. Nor did Pettigrew smile now. 'I'm sorry,' Peabody said. 'Try to forget it.' He said: 'We decided to name her Jefferson.' Now Pettigrew didn't seem to breathe even. He just stood there, small, frail, less than boy-size, childless and bachelor, incorrigibly kinless and tieless, looking at Peabody. Then he breathed, and raising the brush, he turned back to the horse and for an instant Peabody thought he was going back to the grooming. But instead of making the stroke, he laid the hand and the brush against the horse's flank and stood for a moment, his face turned away and his head bent a little. Then he raised his head and turned his face back toward Peabody.

'You could call that lock "axle-grease" on that Indian account,' he said.

'Fifty dollars' worth of axle-grease?' Peabody said.

'To grease the wagons for Oklahoma,' Pettigrew said.

'So we could,' Peabody said. 'Only her name's Jefferson now. We can't ever forget that any more now.' And that was the courthouse—the courthouse which it had taken them almost thirty years not only to realise they didn't have, but to discover that they hadn't even needed, missed, lacked; and which, before they had owned it six months, they discovered was nowhere near enough. Because somewhere between the dark of that first day and the dawn of the next, something happened to them. They began that same day; they restored the jail wall and cut new logs and split out shakes and raised the little floorless lean-to against it and moved the iron chest from Ratcliffe's back room; it took only the two days and cost nothing but the labour and not much of that per capita since the whole settlement was involved to a man, not to mention the settlement's two slaves—Holston's man and the one belonging to the German blacksmith—; Ratcliffe too, all he had to do was put up the bar across the inside of his back door, since his entire patronage was countable in one glance sweating and cursing among the logs and shakes of the half dismantled jail across the way opposite —including Ikkemotubbe's Chickasaw, though these were neither sweating nor cursing: the grave dark men dressed in their Sunday clothes except for the trousers, pants, which they carried rolled neatly under their arms or perhaps tied by the two legs around their necks like capes or rather hussars' dolmans where they had forded the creek,

B

squatting or lounging along the shade, courteous, interested, and reposed (even old Mohataha herself, the matriarch, barefoot in a purple silk gown and a plumed hat,
sitting in a gilt brocade empire chair in a wagon behind
two mules, under a silver-handled Paris parasol held by a
female slave child)—because they (the other white men,
his confreres, or—during this first day—his co-victims)
had not yet remarked the thing—quality—something—
esoteric, eccentric, in Ratcliffe's manner, attitude,—not
an obstruction nor even an impediment, not even when
on the second day they discovered what it was, because
he was among them, busy too, sweating and cursing too,
but rather like a single chip, infinitesimal, on an otherwise
unbroken flood or tide, a single body or substance, alien
and unreconciled, a single thin almost unheard voice cry-
ing thinly out of the roar of a mob: 'Wait, look here,
listen——'

Because they were too busy raging and sweating among
the dismantled logs and felling the new ones in the adjacent
woods and trimming and notching and dragging them
out and mixing the tenuous clay mud to chink them
together with; it was not until the second day that they
learned what was troubling Ratcliffe, because now they
had time, the work going no slower, no lessening of
sweat but on the contrary, if anything the work going
even a little faster because now there was a lightness in the
speed and all that was abated was the rage and the outrage, because somewhere between the dark and the dawn
of the first and the second day, something had happened
to them—the men who had spent that first long hot endless July day sweating and raging about the wrecked jail,

flinging indiscriminately and savagely aside the dismantled logs and the log-like laudanum-smitten inmates in order to rebuild the one, cursing old Holston and the lock and the four—three—bandits and the eleven militiamen who had arrested them, and Compson and Pettigrew and Peabody and the United States of America—the same men met at the project before sunrise on the next day which was already promising to be hot and endless too, but with the rage and the fury absent now, quiet, not grave so much as sobered, a little amazed, diffident, blinking a little perhaps, looking a little aside from one another, a little unfamiliar even to one another in the new jonquil-coloured light, looking about them at the meagre huddle of crude cabins set without order and every one a little awry to every other and all dwarfed to doll-houses by the vast loom of the woods which enclosed them—the tiny clearing clawed punily not even into the flank of pathless wilderness but into the loin, the groin, the secret parts, which was the irrevocable cast die of their lives, fates, pasts and futures—not even speaking for a while yet since each one probably believed (a little shamefaced too) that the thought was solitarily his, until at last one spoke for all and then it was all right since it had taken one conjoined breath to shape that sound, the speaker speaking not loud, diffidently, tentatively, as you insert the first light tentative push of wind into the mouthpiece of a strange untried foxhorn: 'By God. Jefferson.'

'Jefferson, Mississippi,' a second added.

'Jefferson, Yoknapatawpha County, Mississippi,' a third corrected; who, which one, didn't matter this time either since it was still one conjoined breathing, one compound dream-state, mused and static, well capable of lasting on past sunrise too, though they probably knew better too since Compson was still there: the gnat, the thorn, the catalyst.

'It ain't until we finish the goddamned thing,' Compson said. 'Come on. Let's get at it.' So they finished it that day, working rapidly now, with speed and lightness too, concentrated yet inattentive, to get it done and that quickly, not to finish it but to get it out of the way, behind them; not to finish it quickly in order to own, possess it sooner, but to be able to obliterate, efface, it the sooner, as if they had also known in that first yellow light that it would not be near enough, would not even be the beginning; that the little lean-to room they were building would not even be a pattern and could not even be called practice, working on until noon, the hour to stop and eat, by which time Louis Grenier had arrived from Frenchman's Bend (his plantation: his manor, his kitchens and stables and kennels and slave quarters and gardens and promenades and fields which a hundred years later will have vanished, his name and his blood too, leaving nothing but the name of his plantation and his own fading corrupted legend like a thin layer of the native ephemeral yet inevictable dust on a section of country surrounding a little lost paintless crossroads store) twenty miles away behind a slave coachman and footman in his imported English carriage and what was said to be the finest matched team outside of Natchez or Nashville, and Compson said, 'I reckon that'll do'—all knowing what he meant: not abandonment: to complete it, of course, but so little remained now that the two slaves could finish it. The four in fact, since, although as soon as it was assumed that the two Grenier Negroes would lend

the two local ones a hand, Compson demurred on the
grounds that who would dare violate the rigid protocol
of bondage by ordering a stable-servant, let alone a house-
servant, to do manual labour, not to mention having the
temerity to approach old Louis Grenier with the sug-
gestion, Peabody nipped that at once.

'One of them can use my shadow,' he said. 'It
never blenched out there with a white doctor standing in
it,' and even offered to be emissary to old Grenier, except
that Grenier himself forestalled them. So they ate Holston's noon ordinary, while the Chickasaws, squatting
unmoving still where the creep of shade had left them in
the full fierce glare of July noon about the wagon where
old Mohataha still sat under her slave-borne Paris parasol,
ate their lunches too which (Mohataha's and her personal
retinue's came out of a woven whiteoak withe fishbasket
in the wagonbed) they appeared to have carried in from
what, patterning the white people, they called their
plantation too, under their arms inside the rolled-up
trousers. Then they moved back to the front gallery and
—not the settlement any more now: the town; it had been
a town for thirty-one hours now—watched the four slaves
put up the final log and pin down the final shake on the
roof and hang the door, and then, Ratcliffe leading something like the court chamberlain across a castle courtyard,
cross back to the store and enter and emerge carrying the
iron chest, the grave Chickasaws watching too the white
man's slaves sweating the white man's ponderable dense
inscrutable medicine into its new shrine. And now they
had time to find out what was bothering Ratcliffe.

'That lock,' Ratcliffe said.

'What?' somebody said.

'That Indian axle-grease,' Ratcliffe said.

'What?' they said again. But they knew, understood, now. It was neither lock nor axle-grease; it was the fifteen dollars which could have been charged to the Indian Department on Ratcliffe's books and nobody would have ever found it, noticed it, missed it. It was not greed on Ratcliffe's part, and least of all was he advocating corruption. The idea was not even new to him; it did not need any casual man on a horse riding in to the settlement once every two or three weeks, to reveal to him that possibility; he had thought of that the first time he had charged the first sack of peppermint candy to the first one of old Mohataha's forty-year-old grandchildren and had refrained from adding two zeroes to the ten or fifteen cents for ten years now, wondering each time why he did refrain, amazed at his own virtue or at least his strength of will. It was a matter of principle. It was he—they: the settlement (town now)—who had thought of charging the lock to the United States as a provable lock, a communal risk, a concrete ineradicable object, win lose or draw, let the chips fall where they may, on that dim day when some Federal inspector might, just barely might, audit the Chickasaw affairs; it was the United States itself which had voluntarily offered to show them how to transmute the inevictable lock into proofless and ephemeral axle-grease—the little scrawny child-sized man, solitary unarmed impregnable and unalarmed, not even defying them, not even advocate and representative of the United States, but *the* United States, as though the United States had said, 'Please accept a gift of fifteen dollars' (the town had actually paid old Alec fifteen dollars for the lock; he would accept no more), and they had not even declined it but simply abolished it since, as soon as Pettigrew breathed it into sound, the United States had already forever lost it; as though Pettigrew had put the actual ponderable fifteen gold coins into—say, Compson's or Peabody's—hands and they had dropped them down a rat-hole or a well, doing no man any good, neither restoration to the ravaged nor emolument to the ravager, leaving in fact the whole race of man, as long as it endured, forever and irrevocably fifteen dollars deficit, fifteen dollars in the red;

That was Ratcliffe's trouble. But they didn't even listen. They heard him out of course, but they didn't even listen. Or perhaps they didn't even hear him either, sitting along the shade on Holston's gallery, looking, seeing, already a year away; it was barely the tenth of July; there was the long summer, the bright soft dry fall until the November rains, but they would require not two days this time but two years and maybe more, with a winter of planning and preparation before hand. They even had an instrument available and waiting, like providence almost: a man named Sutpen who had come into the settlement that same spring—a big gaunt friendless passion-worn untalkative man who walked in a fading aura of anonymity and violence like a man just entered a warm room or at least a shelter, out of a blizzard, bringing with him thirty-odd men slaves even wilder and more equivocal than the native wild men, the Chickasaws, to whom the settlement had become accustomed, who (the new Negroes) spoke no English but instead what Compson, who had visited New Orleans, said was the Carib-Spanish-French of the Sugar Islands, and who (Sutpen) had bought or proved on or

anyway acquired a tract of land in the opposite direction
and was apparently bent on establishing a place on an even
more ambitious and grandiose scale than Grenier's; he had
even brought with him a tame Parisian architect—or cap-
tive rather, since it was said in Ratcliffe's back room that
the man slept at night in a kind of pit at the site of the
chateau he was planning, tied wrist to wrist with one of
his captor's Carib slaves; indeed, the settlement had only
to see him once to know that he was no dociler than his
captor, any more than the weasel or rattlesnake is no less
untame than the wolf or bear before which it gives way
until completely and hopelessly cornered:—a man no
larger than Pettigrew, with humorous sardonic undefeated
eyes which had seen everything and believed none of it,
in the broad expensive hat and brocaded waistcoat and
ruffled wrists of a half-artist half-boulevardier; and they—
Compson perhaps, Peabody certainly—could imagine
him in his mudstained brier-slashed brocade and lace
standing in a trackless wilderness dreaming colonnades
and porticoes and fountains and promenades in the style
of David, with just behind each elbow an identical giant
half-naked Negro not even watching him, only breathing,
moving each time he took a step or shifted like his shadow
repeated in two and blown to gigantic size;

So they even had an architect. He listened to them for
perhaps a minute in Ratcliffe's back room. Then he made
an indescribable gesture and said, 'Bah. You do not need
advice. You are too poor. You have only your hands, and
clay to make good brick. You don't have any money.
You don't even have anything to copy: how can you go
wrong?' But he taught them how to mould the brick; he

designed and built the kiln to bake the brick in, plenty of them since they had probably known from that first yellow morning too that one edifice was not going to be enough. But although both were conceived in the same instant and planned simultaneously during the same winter and built in continuation during the next three years, the courthouse of course came first, and in March, with stakes and hanks of fishline, the architect laid out in a grove of oaks opposite the tavern and the store, the square and simple foundations, the irrevocable design not only of the courthouse but of the town too, telling them as much: 'In fifty years you will be trying to change it in the name of what you will call progress. But you will fail; but you will never be able to get away from it.' But they had already seen that, standing thigh-deep in wilderness also but with more than a vision to look at since they had at least the fish-line and the stakes, perhaps less than fifty years, perhaps—who knew?—less than twenty-five even: a Square, the courthouse in its grove the centre; quadrangular around it, the stores, two-storey, the offices of the lawyers and doctors and dentists, the lodge-rooms and auditoriums, above them; school and church and tavern and bank and jail each in its ordered place; the four broad diverging avenues straight as plumb-lines in the four directions, becoming the network of roads and by-roads until the whole county would be covered with it: the hands, the prehensile fingers clawing dragging lightward out of the disappearing wilderness year by year as up from the bottom of the receding sea, the broad rich fecund burgeoning fields, pushing thrusting each year further and further back the wilderness and its denizens—the wild bear and deer and turkey, and the wild men (or not so

wild any more, familiar now, harmless now, just obsolete: anachronism out of an old dead time and a dead age;
regrettable of course, even actually regretted by the old
men, fiercely as old Doctor Habersham did, and with less
fire but still as irreconcilable and stubborn as old Alec
Holston and a few others were still doing, until in a few
more years the last of them would have passed and vanished in their turn too, obsolescent too: because this was
a white man's land; that was its fate, or not even fate but
destiny, its high destiny in the roster of the earth)—the
veins, arteries, life- and pulse-stream along which would
flow the aggrandisement of harvest: the gold: the cotton
and the grain;

But above all, the courthouse: the centre, the focus, the
hub; sitting looming in the centre of the county's circumference like a single cloud in its ring of horizon, laying its
vast shadow to the uttermost rim of horizon; musing,
brooding, symbolic and ponderable, tall as cloud, solid as
rock, dominating all: protector of the weak, judiciate and
curb of the passions and lusts, repository and guardian of
the aspirations and the hopes; rising course by brick
course during that first summer, simply square, simplest
Georgian colonial (this, by the Paris architect who was
creating at Sutpen's Hundred something like a wing of
Versailles glimpsed in a Lilliput's gothic nightmare—in
revenge, Gavin Stevens would say a hundred years later,
when Sutpen's own legend in the county would include
the anecdote of the time the architect broke somehow out
of his dungeon and tried to flee and Sutpen and his Negro
head man and hunter ran him down with dogs in the
swamp and brought him back) since, as the architect had

told them, they had no money to buy bad taste with nor even anything from which to copy what bad taste might still have been within their compass; this one too still costing nothing but the labour and—the second year now—most of that was slave since there were still more slave owners in the settlement which had been a town and named for going on two years now, already a town and already named when the first ones waked up on that yellow morning two years back:—men other than Holston and the blacksmith (Compson was one now) who owned one or two or three Negroes, besides Grenier and Sutpen who had set up camps beside the creek in Compson's pasture for the two gangs of their Negroes to live in until the two buildings—the courthouse and the jail—should be completed. But not altogether slave, the bound-men, the unfree, because there were still the white men too, the same ones who on that hot July morning two and now three years ago had gathered in a kind of outraged unbelief to fling, hurl up in raging sweating impotent fury the little three-walled lean-to—the same men (with affairs of their own they might have been attending to or work of their own or for which they were being hired, paid, that they should have been doing) standing or lounging about the scaffolding and the stacks of brick and puddles of clay mortar for an hour or two hours or half a day, then putting aside one of the Negroes and taking his place with trowel or saw or adze, unbidden or unreproved either since there was none present with the right to order or deny; a stranger might have said probably for that reason, simply because now they didn't have to, except that it was more than that, working peacefully now that there was no outrage and fury, and twice as fast because there

was no urgency since this was no more to be hurried by
man or men than the burgeoning of a crop, working (this
paradox too to anyone except men like Grenier and
Compson and Peabody who had grown from infancy
among slaves, breathed the same air and even suckled the
same breast with the sons of Ham: black and white, free
and unfree, shoulder to shoulder in the same tireless lift
and rhythm as if they had the same aim and hope, which
they did have as far as the Negro was capable, as even
Ratcliffe, son of a long pure line of Anglo-Saxon moun-
tain people and—destined—father of an equally long and
pure line of white trash tenant farmers who never owned
a slave and never would since each had and would imbibe
with his mother's milk a personal violent antipathy not at
all to slavery but to black skins, could have explained: the
slave's simple child's mind had fired at once with the
thought that he was helping to build not only the biggest
edifice in the country, but probably the biggest he had
ever seen; this was all but this was enough) as one because
it was theirs, bigger than any because it was the sum of
all and, being the sum of all, it must raise all of their hopes
and aspirations level with its own aspirant and soaring
cupola, so that, sweating and tireless and unflagging, they
would look about at one another a little shyly, a little
amazed, with something like humility too, as if they were
realising, or were for a moment at least capable of believing, that men, all men, including themselves, were a little
better, purer maybe even, than they had thought, expected, or even needed to be. Though they were still having
a little trouble with Ratcliffe: the money, the Holston
lock-Chickasaw axle-grease fifteen dollars; not trouble
really because it had never been an obstruction even three

years ago when it was new, and now after three years
even the light impedeless chip was worn by familiarity
and custom to less than a toothpick: merely present, merely
visible, or that is, audible: and no trouble *with* Ratcliffe
because he made one too contraposed the tooth-pick;
more: he was its chief victim, sufferer, since where with
the others was mostly inattention, a little humour, now
and then a little fading annoyance and impatience, with
him was shame, bafflement, a little of anguish and despair
like a man struggling with a congenital vice, hopeless,
indomitable, already defeated. It was not even the money
any more now, the fifteen dollars. It was the fact that they
had refused it and, refusing it, had maybe committed a
fatal and irremediable error. He would try to explain it:
'It's like Old Moster and the rest of them up there that
run the luck, would look down at us and say, Well well,
looks like them durn peckerwoods down there don't want
them fifteen dollars we was going to give them free-
gratis-for-nothing. So maybe they don't want nothing
from us. So maybe we better do like they seem to want,
and let them sweat and swivet and scrabble through the
best they can by themselves.'

Which they—the town—did, though even then the courthouse was not finished for another six years. Not but
that they thought it was: complete: simple and square,
floored and roofed and windowed, with a central hallway
and the four offices—sheriff and tax assessor and circuit-
and chancery-clerk (which—the chancery-clerk's office—
would contain the ballot boxes and booths for voting)
—below, and the courtroom and jury-room and the
judge's chambers above—even to the pigeons and English

sparrows, migrants too but not pioneers, inevictably urban in fact, come all the way from the Atlantic coast as soon as the town became a town with a name, taking possession of the gutters and eave-boxes almost before the final hammer was withdrawn, uxorious and interminable the one, garrulous and myriad the other. Then in the sixth year old Alec Holston died and bequeathed back to the town the fifteen dollars it had paid him for the lock; two years before, Louis Grenier had died and his heirs still held in trust on demand the fifteen hundred dollars his will had devised it, and now there was another newcomer in the county, a man named John Sartoris, with slaves and gear and money too like Grenier and Sutpen, but who was an even better stalemate to Sutpen than Grenier had been because it was apparent at once that he, Sartoris, was the sort of man who could even cope with Sutpen in the sense that a man with a sabre or even a small sword and heart enough for it could cope with one with an axe; and that summer (Sutpen's Paris architect had long since gone back to whatever place he came from and to which he had made his one abortive midnight try to return, but his trickle, flow of bricks had never even faltered: his moulds and kilns had finished the jail and were now raising the walls of two churches and by the half-century would have completed what would be known through all north Mississippi and east Tennessee as *the* Academy, *the* Female Institute) there was a committee: Compson and Sartoris and Peabody (and *in absentia* Sutpen: nor would the town ever know exactly how much of the additional cost Sutpen and Sartoris made up): and the next year the eight disjointed marble columns were landed from an Italian ship at New Orleans, into a

steamboat up the Mississippi to Vicksburg, and into a
smaller steamboat up the Yazoo and Sunflower and Tal-
lahatchie, to Ikkemotubbe's old landing which Sutpen
now owned, and thence the twelve miles by oxen into
Jefferson: the two identical four-column porticoes, one
on the north and one on the south, each with its balcony
of wrought-iron New Orleans grillwork, on one of
which—the south one—in 1861 Sartoris would stand in
the first Confederate uniform the town had ever seen,
while in the Square below the Richmond mustering
officer enrolled and swore in the regiment which Sartoris
as its colonel would take to Virginia as a part of Bee,
to be Jackson's extreme left in front of the Henry house
at First Manassas, and from both of which each May
and November for a hundred years, bailiffs in their
orderly appointive almost hereditary succession would
cry without inflection or punctuation either 'oyes oyes
honourable circuit court of Yoknapatawpha County
come all and ye shall be heard' and beneath which for
that same length of time too except for the seven years
between '63 and '70 which didn't really count a century
afterward except to a few irreconcilable old ladies, the
white male citizens of the county would pass to vote for
county and state offices, because when in '63 a United
States military force burned the Square and the business
district, the courthouse survived. It didn't escape: it simply
survived: harder than axes, tougher than fire, more fixed
than dynamite; encircled by the tumbled and blackened
ruins of lesser walls, it still stood, even the topless smoke-
stained columns, gutted of course and roofless, but immune, not one hair even out of the Paris architect's almost
forgotten plumb, so that all they had to do (it took nine

years to build; they needed twenty-five to restore it) was
put in new floors for the two storeys and a new roof, and
this time with a cupola with a four-faced clock and a bell
to strike the hours and ring alarms; by this time the
Square, the banks and the stores and the lawyers' and
doctors' and dentists' offices, had been restored, and the
English sparrows were back too which had never really
deserted—the garrulous noisy independent swarms which,
as though concomitant with, inextricable from regular-
ised and roted human quarrelling, had appeared in possession of cornices and gutter-boxes almost before the last
nail was driven—and now the pigeons also, interminably
murmurous, nesting in, already usurping, the belfry even
though they couldn't seem to get used to the bell, bursting
out of the cupola at each stroke of the hour in frantic
clouds, to sink and burst and whirl again at each succeed-
ing stroke, until the last one: then vanishing back through
the slatted louvres until nothing remained but the frantic
and murmurous cooing like the fading echoes of the bell
itself, the source of the alarm never recognised and even
the alarm itself unremembered, as the actual stroke of
the bell is no longer remembered by the vibration-fading
air. Because they—the sparrows and the pigeons—endured, durable, a hundred years, the oldest things there
except the courthouse centennial and serene above the
town most of whose people now no longer even knew
who Doctor Habersham and old Alec Holston and Louis
Grenier were, had been; centennial and serene above the
change: the electricity and gasolene, the neon and the
crowded cacophonous air; even Negroes passing in beneath the balconies and into the chancery clerk's office to
cast ballots too, voting for the same white-skinned rascals

and demagogues and white supremacy champions that the white ones did—durable: every few years the county fathers, dreaming of baksheesh, would instigate a movement to tear it down and erect a new modern one, but someone would at the last moment defeat them; they will try it again of course and be defeated perhaps once again or even maybe twice again, but no more than that. Because its fate is to stand in the hinterland of America: its doom is its longevity; like a man, its simple age is its own reproach, and after the hundred years, will become unbearable. But not for a little while yet; for a little while yet the sparrows and the pigeons: garrulous myriad and independent the one, the other uxorious and interminable, at once frantic and tranquil—until the clock strikes again which even after a hundred years, they still seem unable to get used to, bursting in one swirling explosion out of the belfry as though the hour, instead of merely adding one puny infinitesimal more to the long weary increment since Genesis, had shattered the virgin pristine air with the first loud ding-dong of time and doom.

Courtroom. 5.30 P.M. November thirteenth.

The curtain is down. As the lights begin to go up:

MAN'S VOICE
(behind the curtain)
Let the prisoner stand.

The curtain rises, symbolising the rising of the prisoner
in the dock, and revealing a section of the courtroom. It
does not occupy the whole stage, but only the upper left
half, leaving the other half and the bottom of the stage
in darkness, so that the visible scene is not only spot-
lighted but elevated slightly too, a further symbolism
which will be clearer when Act II opens—the symbolism
of the elevated tribunal of justice of which this, a county
court, is only the intermediate, not the highest, stage.

This is a section of the court—the bar, the judge, officers, the opposing lawyers, the jury. The defence lawyer
is Gavin Stevens, about fifty. He looks more like a poet
than a lawyer and actually is: a bachelor, descendant
of one of the pioneer Yoknapatawpha County families,
Harvard and Heidelberg educated, and returned to his
native soil to be a sort of bucolic Cincinnatus, champion
not so much of truth as of justice, or of justice as he sees
it, constantly involving himself, often for no pay, in
affairs of equity and passion and even crime too among
his people, white and Negro both, sometimes directly
contrary to his office of County Attorney which he has
held for years, as is the present business.

The prisoner is standing. She is the only one standing in the room—a Negress, quite black, about thirty—that is, she could be almost anything between twenty and forty —with a calm impenetrable almost bemused face, the tallest, highest there with all eyes on her but she herself not looking at any of them, but looking out and up as though at some distant corner of the room, as though she were alone in it. She is—or was until recently, five months ago to be exact—a domestic servant, nurse to two white children, the second of whom, an infant, she smothered in its cradle five months ago, for which act she is now on trial for her life. But she has probably done many things else—chopped cotton, cooked for working gangs—any sort of manual labour within her capacities, or rather, limitations in time and availability, since her principal reputation in the little Mississippi town where she was born is that of a tramp—a drunkard, a casual prostitute, being beaten by some man or cutting or being cut by his wife or his other sweetheart. She has probably been married, at least once. Her name—or so she calls it and would probably spell it if she could spell—is Nancy Mannigoe.

There is a dead silence in the room while everybody watches her.

JUDGE

Have you anything to say before the sentence of the court is pronounced upon you?

Nancy neither answers nor moves; she doesn't even seem to be listening.

That you, Nancy Mannigoe, did on the ninth day of September, wilfully and with malice afore-thought kill and murder the infant child of Mr.

and Mrs. Gowan Stevens in the town of Jefferson
and the County of Yoknapatawpha . . .

It is the sentence of this court that you be taken
from hence back to the county jail of Yoknapatawpha County and there on the thirteenth day of
March be hanged by the neck until you are dead.
And may God have mercy on your soul.

NANCY
(quite loud in the silence, to no one, quite
calm, not moving)
Yes, Lord.

There is a gasp, a sound, from the invisible spectators in
the room, of shock at this unheard-of violation of pro-
cedure: the beginning of something which might be con-
sternation and even uproar, in the midst of, or rather
above which, Nancy herself does not move. The judge
bangs his gavel, the bailiff springs up, the curtain starts
hurriedly and jerkily down as if the judge, the officers,
the court itself were jerking frantically at it to hide this
disgraceful business; from somewhere among the unseen
spectators there comes the sound of a woman's voice—
a moan, wail, sob perhaps.

BAILIFF
(loudly)
Order! Order in the court! Order!

The curtain descends rapidly, hiding the scene, the lights
fade rapidly into darkness: a moment of darkness: then
the curtain rises smoothly and normally on:

Stevenses' living-room. 6.00 P.M. November thirteenth.

Living-room, a centre table with a lamp, chairs, a sofa
left rear, floor-lamp, wall-bracket lamps, a door left enters
from the hall, double doors rear stand open on a dining-
room, a fireplace right with gas logs. The atmosphere of
the room is smart, modern, up-to-date, yet the room
itself has the air of another time—the high ceiling, the
cornices, some of the furniture; it has the air of being in an
old house, an ante-bellum house descended at last to a
spinster survivor who has modernised it (vide the gas fire
and the two overstuffed chairs) into apartments rented to
young couples or families who can afford to pay that
much rent in order to live on the right street among
other young couples who belong to the right church and
the country club.

Sound of feet, then the lights come on as if someone
about to enter had pressed a wall switch, then the door
left opens and Temple enters, followed by Gowan, her
husband, and the lawyer, Gavin Stevens. She is in the
middle twenties, very smart, soignée, in an open fur coat,
wearing a hat and gloves and carrying a handbag. Her air
is brittle and tense, yet controlled. Her face shows nothing
as she crosses to the centre table and stops. Gowan is three
or four years older. He is almost a type; there were many
of him in America, the South, between the two great
wars: only children of financially secure parents living in
city apartment hotels, alumni of the best colleges, South
or East, where they belonged to the right clubs; married
now and raising families yet still alumni of their schools,

53

performing acceptably jobs they themselves did not ask for, usually concerned with money: cotton futures, or stocks, or bonds. But this face is a little different, a little more than that. Something has happened to it—tragedy— something, against which it had had no warning, and to cope with which (as it discovered) no equipment, yet which it has accepted and is trying, really and sincerely and selflessly (perhaps for the first time in its life) to do its best with according to its code. He and Stevens wear their overcoats, carrying their hats. Stevens stops just inside the room. Gowan drops his hat onto the sofa in passing and goes on to where Temple stands at the table, stripping off one of her gloves.

TEMPLE
(takes cigarette from box on the table: mimics the prisoner; her voice, harsh, reveals for the first time repressed, controlled, hysteria)
Yes, God. Guilty, God. Thank you, God. If that's your attitude toward being hung, what else can you expect from a judge and jury except to accommodate you?

GOWAN
Stop it, Boots. Hush now. Soon as I light the fire, I'll buy a drink.
(to Stevens)
Or maybe Gavin will do the fire while I do the butler.

TEMPLE
(takes up lighter)
I'll do the fire. You get the drinks. Then Uncle

Gavin won't have to stay. After all, all he wants
to do is say good-bye and send me a postcard. He
can almost do that in two words, if he tries hard.
Then he can go home.

She crosses to the hearth and kneels and turns the gas
valve, the lighter ready in her other hand.

                    GOWAN
                  (anxiously)
Now, Boots.

                    TEMPLE
          (snaps lighter, holds flame to the jet)
Will you for God's sake please get me a drink?

                    GOWAN
Sure, honey.
                  (he turns: to Stevens)
Drop your coat anywhere.

He exits into the dining-room. Stevens does not move,
watching Temple as the log takes fire.

                    TEMPLE
          (still kneeling, her back to Stevens)
If you're going to stay, why don't you sit down?
Or vice versa. Backward. Only, it's the first one
that's backward: if you're not sitting down, why
don't you go? Let me be bereaved and vindicated,
but at least let me do it in privacy, since God
knows if any one of the excretions should take
place in privacy, triumph should be the one——

Stevens watches her. Then he crosses to her, taking the
handkerchief from his breast pocket, stops behind her
and extends the handkerchief down where she can see

it. She looks at it, then up at him. Her face is quite calm.

TEMPLE
What's that for?

STEVENS
It's all right. It's dry too.
(still extending the handkerchief)
For tomorrow, then.

TEMPLE
(rises quickly)
Oh, for cinders. On the train. We're going by air; hadn't Gowan told you? We leave from the Memphis airport at midnight; we're driving up after supper. Then California tomorrow morning; maybe we'll even go on to Hawaii in the spring. No; wrong season: Canada, maybe. Lake Louise in May and June——
(she stops, listens a moment toward the dining-room doors)
So why the handkerchief? Not a threat, because you don't have anything to threaten me with, do you? And if you don't have anything to threaten me with, I must not have anything you want, so it can't be a bribe either, can it?
(they both hear the sound from beyond the dining-room doors which indicates that Gowan is approaching. Temple lowers her voice again, rapidly)
Put it this way then. I don't know what you want, because I don't care. Because whatever it is, you won't get it from me.

> (the sound is near now—footsteps, clink
> of glass)

Now he'll offer you a drink, and then he'll ask
you too what you want, why you followed us
home. I've already answered you. No. If what you
came for is to see me weep, I doubt if you'll even
get that. But you certainly won't get anything
else. Not from me. Do you understand that?

STEVENS

I hear you.

TEMPLE

Meaning, you don't believe it. All right, *touché*
then.

> (quicker, tenser)

I refused to answer your question; now I'll ask
you one: How much do you—

> (as Gowan enters, she changes what she
> was saying so smoothly in mid-sentence
> that anyone entering would not even
> realise that the pitch of her voice had
> altered)

—are her lawyer, she must have talked to you;
even a dope-fiend that murders a little baby must
have what she calls some excuse for it, even a
nigger dope-fiend and a white baby—or maybe
even more, a nigger dope-fiend and a white
baby——

GOWAN

I said, stop it, Boots.

He carries a tray containing a pitcher of water, a bowl
of ice, three empty tumblers and three whiskey glasses

already filled. The bottle itself protrudes from his top-coat pocket. He approaches Temple and offers the tray.

>That's right. I'm going to have one myself. For a change. After eight years. Why not?

TEMPLE

Why not?
>(looks at the tray)

Not highballs?

GOWAN

Not this one.

She takes one of the filled glasses. He offers the tray to Stevens, who takes the second one. Then he sets the tray on the table and takes up the third glass.

>Nary a drink in eight years; count 'em. So maybe this will be a good time to start again. At least, it won't be too soon.
>(to Stevens)

Drink up. A little water behind it?

As though not aware that he had done so, he sets his untasted glass back on the tray, splashes water from the pitcher into a tumbler and hands the tumbler to Stevens as Stevens empties his glass and lowers it, taking the tumbler. Temple has not touched hers either.

>Now maybe Defence Attorney Stevens will tell us what he wants here.

STEVENS

Your wife has already told you. To say good-bye.

GOWAN

Then say it. One more for the road, and where's your hat, huh?

He takes the tumbler from Stevens and turns back to the table.

                    TEMPLE
          (sets her untasted glass back on the tray)
And put ice in it this time, and maybe even a little water. But first, take Uncle Gavin's coat.

                    GOWAN
          (takes bottle from his pocket and makes
          a highball for Stevens in the tumbler)
That won't be necessary. If he could raise his arm in a white courtroom to defend a murdering nigger, he can certainly bend it in nothing but a wool overcoat—at least to take a drink with the victim's mother.
          (quickly: to Temple)
Sorry. Maybe you were right all the time, and I was wrong. Maybe we've both got to keep on saying things like that until we can get rid of them, some of them, a little of them——

                    TEMPLE
All right, why not? Here goes then.
          (she is watching, not Gowan but Stevens,
          who watches her in return, grave and
          soberly)
Don't forget the father too, dear.

                    GOWAN
          (mixing the drink)
Why should I, dear? How could I, dear? Except that the child's father is unfortunately just a man. In the eyes of the law, men are not supposed to

suffer: they are merely appellants or appellees. The law is tender only of women and children—particularly of women, particularly particular of nigger dope-fiend whores who murder white children.

> (hands the highball to Stevens, who takes it)

So why should we expect Defence Attorney Stevens to be tender of a man or a woman who just happen to be the parents of the child that got murdered?

TEMPLE
(harshly)

Will you for God's sake please get through? Then will you for God's sake please hush?

GOWAN
(quickly: turns)

Sorry.

> (he turns toward her, sees her hand empty, then sees her full glass beside his own on the tray)

No drink?

TEMPLE
I don't want it. I want some milk.

GOWAN
Right. Hot, of course.

TEMPLE
Please.

GOWAN
(turning)

Right. I thought of that too. I put a pan on to

heat while I was getting the drinks.
            (crossing toward dining-room exit)
Don't let Uncle Gavin get away until I get back.
Lock the door, if you have to. Or maybe just
telephone that nigger freedom agent—what's his
name?——

He exits. They don't move until the slap of the pantry
door sounds.

TEMPLE
            (rapid and hard)
How much do you know?
            (rapidly)
Don't lie to me; don't you see there's not time?

STEVENS
Not time for what? Before your plane leaves
tonight? She has a little time yet—four months,
until March, the thirteenth of March——

TEMPLE
You know what I mean—her lawyer—seeing her
every day—just a nigger, and you a white man
—even if you needed anything to frighten her with
—you could just buy it from her with a dose of
cocaine or a pint of . . .
            (she stops, stares at him, in a sort of
            amazement, despair; her voice is almost
            quiet)
Oh, God, oh, God, she hasn't told you anything.
It's me; I'm the one that's—— Don't you see?
It's that I cannot believe—will not believe—
impossible——

STEVENS

Impossible to believe that all human beings really
don't—as you would put it—stink? Even—as you
put it—dope-fiend nigger whores? No, she told
me nothing more.

TEMPLE
(prompts)
Even if there was anything more.

STEVENS

Even if there was.

TEMPLE

Then what is it you think you know? Never mind
where you got it; just tell me what you think it is.

STEVENS

There was a man there that night.

TEMPLE
(quick, glib, almost before he has finished)
Gowan.

STEVENS

That night? When Gowan had left with Bucky at
six that morning to drive to New Orleans in a car?

TEMPLE
(quick, harsh)
So I was right. Did you frighten her, or just buy it?
(interrupts herself)
I'm trying. I'm really trying. Maybe it wouldn't
be so hard if I could just understand why they
don't stink—what reason they would have for not
stinking. . . .

(she stops; it is as if she had heard a sound
presaging Gowan's return, or perhaps
simply knew by instinct or from knowledge of her own house that he had had
time to heat a cup of milk. Then continues, rapid and quiet)

There was no man there. You see? I told you,
warned you, that you would get nothing from me.
Oh, I know; you could have put me on the stand
at any time, under oath; of course, your jury
wouldn't have liked it—that wanton crucifixion
of a bereaved mamma, but what's that in the
balance with justice? I don't know why you didn't.
Or maybe you still intend to—provided you can
catch us before we cross the Tennessee line tonight.

(quick, tense, hard)

All right. I'm sorry. I know better. So maybe it's
just my own stinking after all that I find impossible
to doubt.

(the pantry door slaps again; they both
hear it)

Because I'm not even going to take Gowan with
me when I say good-bye and go up stairs.—And
who knows——

She stops. Gowan enters, carrying a small tray bearing
a glass of milk, a salt-shaker and a napkin, and comes to
the table.

GOWAN

What are you talking about now?

TEMPLE

Nothing. I was telling Uncle Gavin that he had

something of Virginia or some sort of gentleman
in him too that he must have inherited from you
through your grandfather, and that I'm going up
to give Bucky his bath and supper.

> (she touches the glass for heat, then takes
> it up: to Gowan)

Thank you, dear.

GOWAN

Right, dear.

> (to Stevens)

You see? Not just a napkin: the right napkin.
That's how I'm trained.

> (he stops suddenly, noticing Temple, who
> who has done nothing apparently: just
> standing there holding the milk. But he
> seems to know what is going on: to her)

What's this for?

TEMPLE

I don't know.
He moves; they kiss, not long but not a peck either; defi-
nitely a kiss between a man and a woman. Then, carrying
the milk, Temple crosses toward the hall door.

> (to Stevens)

Good-bye then until next June. Bucky will send you and
Maggie a postcard.

> (she goes on to the door, pauses and
> looks back at Stevens)

I may even be wrong about Temple Drake's odour
too; if you should happen to hear something you
haven't heard yet and it's true, I may even ratify
it. Maybe you can even believe that—if you can

believe you are going to hear anything that you haven't heard yet.

STEVENS
Do you?

TEMPLE
(after a moment)

Not from me, Uncle Gavin. If someone wants to go to heaven, who am I to stop them? Good night. Good-bye.

She exits, closes the door. Stevens, very grave, turns back and sets his highball down on the tray.

GOWAN
Drink up. After all, I've got to eat supper and do some packing too. How about it?

STEVENS
About what? The packing, or the drink? What about you? I thought you were going to have one.

GOWAN
Oh, sure, sure.
(takes up the small filled glass)

Maybe you had better go on and leave us to our revenge.

STEVENS
I wish it could comfort you.

GOWAN
I wish to God it could. I wish to God that what I wanted was only revenge. An eye for an eye— were ever words emptier? Only, you have got to have lost the eye to know it.

C

STEVENS

Yet she still has to die.

GOWAN

Why not? Even if she would be any loss—a nigger whore, a drunkard, a dope-fiend——

STEVENS

—a vagabond, a tramp, hopeless until one day Mr. and Mrs. Gowan Stevens out of simple pity and humanity picked her up out of the gutter to give her one more chance—

> (Gowan stands motionless, his hand tightening slowly about the glass. Stevens watches him)

And then in return for it—

GOWAN

Look, Uncle Gavin. Why don't you go for God's sake home? Or to hell, or anywhere out of here?

STEVENS

I am, in a minute. Is that why you think—why you would still say she has to die?

GOWAN

I don't. I had nothing to do with it. I wasn't even the plaintiff. I didn't even instigate—that's the word, isn't it?—the suit. My only connection with it was, I happened by chance to be the father of the child she—— Who in hell ever called that a drink?

He dashes the whiskey, glass and all, into the ice bowl, quickly catches up one of the empty tumblers in one hand and, at the same time, tilts the whiskey bottle over it, pouring. At first he makes no sound, but at once it is

obvious that he is laughing: laughter which begins normally enough, but almost immediately it is out of hand,
just on hysteria, while he still pours whiskey into the
glass, which in a moment now will overflow, except that
Stevens reaches his hand and grasps the bottle and stops it.

STEVENS
Stop it. Stop it, now. Here.

He takes the bottle from Gowan, sets it down, takes the
tumbler and tilts part of its contents into the other empty
one, leaving at least a reasonable, a believable, drink, and
hands it to Gowan. Gowan takes it, stopping the crazy
laughter, gets hold of himself again.

GOWAN
(holding the glass untasted)

Eight years. Eight years on the wagon—and this
is what I got for it: my child murdered by a dope-
fiend nigger whore that wouldn't even run so that
a cop or somebody could have shot her down like
the mad-dog—You see? Eight years without the
drink, and so I got whatever it was I was buying
by not drinking, and now I've got whatever it was
I was paying for and it's paid for and so I can
drink again. And now I don't want the drink. You
see? Like whatever it was I was buying I not only
didn't want, but what I was paying for it wasn't
worth anything, wasn't even any loss. So I have
a laugh coming. That's triumph. Because I got a
bargain even in what I didn't want. I got a cut
rate. I had two children. I had to pay only one
of them to find out it wasn't really costing me
anything——Half price: a child, and a dope-fiend

nigger whore on a public gallows: that's all I had
to pay for immunity.

STEVENS

There's no such thing.

GOWAN

From the past. From my folly. My drunkenness.
My cowardice, if you like——

STEVENS

There's no such thing as past either.

GOWAN

That is a laugh, that one. Only, not so loud, huh?
to disturb the ladies—disturb Miss Drake—Miss
Temple Drake.—Sure, why not cowardice. Only,
for euphony, call it simple over-training. You
know? Gowan Stevens, trained at Virginia to
drink like a gentleman, gets drunk as ten gentlemen, takes a country college girl, a maiden: who
knows? maybe even a virgin, cross country by car
to another country college ball game, gets drunker
than twenty gentlemen, gets lost, gets still drunker
than forty gentlemen, wrecks the car, passes eighty
gentlemen now, passes completely out while the
maiden the virgin is being kidnapped into a Memphis whorehouse——

> (he mumbles an indistinguishable word)

STEVENS

What?

GOWAN

Sure; cowardice. Call it cowardice; what's a little
euphony between old married people?

STEVENS

Not the marrying her afterward, at least. What——

GOWAN

Sure. Marrying her was purest Old Virginia. That was indeed the hundred and sixty gentlemen.

STEVENS

The intent was, by any other standards too. The prisoner in the whorehouse; I didn't quite hear——

GOWAN
(quickly: reaching for it)
Where's your glass? Dump that slop—here——

STEVENS
(holds glass)
This will do. What was that you said about held prisoner in the whorehouse?

GOWAN
(harshly)
That's all. You heard it.

STEVENS

You said 'and loved it.'
(they stare at each other)
Is that what you can never forgive her for?— not for having been the instrument creating that moment in your life which you can never recall nor forget nor explain nor condone nor even stop thinking about, but because she herself didn't even suffer, but on the contrary, even liked it—that month or whatever it was like the episode in the

old movie of the white girl held prisoner in the cave
by the Bedouin prince?—That you had to lose not
only your bachelor freedom, but your man's self-
respect in the chastity of his wife and your child
too, to pay for something your wife hadn't even
lost, didn't even regret, didn't even miss? Is that
why this poor lost doomed crazy Negro woman
must die?

GOWAN
(tensely)
Get out of here. Go on.

STEVENS
In a minute.—Or else, blow your own brains out:
stop having to remember, stop having to be forever unable to forget: nothing; to plunge into
nothing and sink and drown forever and forever,
never again to have to remember, never again to
wake in the night writhing and sweating because
you cannot, can never, stop remembering?
What else happened during that month, that time
while that madman held her prisoner there in
that Memphis house, that nobody but you and
she know about, maybe not even you know
about?

Still staring at Stevens, slowly and deliberately Gowan
sets the glass of whiskey back on the tray and takes up
the bottle and swings it bottom up back over his head.
The stopper is out, and at once the whiskey begins to
pour out of it, down his arm and sleeve and onto the
floor. He does not seem to be aware of it even. His voice
is tense, barely articulate.

GOWAN
So help me, Christ . . . So help me, Christ.

A moment, then Stevens moves, without haste, sets his own glass back on the tray and turns, taking his hat as he passes the sofa, and goes on to the door and exits. Gowan stands a moment longer with the poised bottle, now empty. Then he draws a long shuddering breath, seems to rouse, wake, sets the empty bottle back on the tray, notices his untasted whiskey glass, takes it up, a moment: then turns and throws the glass crashing into the fireplace, against the burning gas logs, and stands, his back to the audience, and draws another long shuddering breath and then draws both hands hard down his face, then turns, looking at his wet sleeve, takes out his handkerchief and dabs at his sleeve as he comes back to the table, puts the handkerchief back in his pocket and takes the folded napkin from the small tray beside the salt-cellar and wipes his sleeve with it, sees he is doing no good, tosses the crumpled napkin back onto the whiskey tray; and now, outwardly quite calm again, as though nothing had happened, he gathers the glasses back onto the big tray, puts the small tray and the napkin onto it too and takes up the tray and walks quietly toward the dining-room door as the lights begin to go down.

The lights go completely down. The stage is dark.

The lights go up.

Stevenses' living-room. 10.00 P.M. March eleventh.

The room is exactly as it was four months ago, except
that the only light burning is the lamp on the table, and
the sofa has been moved so that it partly faces the audience, with a small motionless blanket-wrapped object
lying on it, and one of the chairs placed between the lamp
and the sofa so that the shadow of its back falls across the
object on the sofa, making it more or less indistinguish-
able, and the dining-room doors are now closed. The
telephone sits on the small stand in the corner right as in
Scene II.

The hall door opens. Temple enters, followed by
Stevens. She now wears a long housecoat; her hair is tied
back with a ribbon as though prepared for bed. This time
Stevens carries the topcoat and the hat too; his suit is
different. Apparently she has already warned Stevens to
be quiet; his air anyway shows it. She enters, stops, lets
him pass her. He pauses, looks about the room, sees the
sofa, stands looking at it.

STEVENS
This is what they call a plant.
He crosses to the sofa, Temple watching him, and stops,
looking down at the shadowed object. He quietly draws
aside the shadowing chair and reveals a little boy, about
four, wrapped in the blanket, asleep.

TEMPLE
Why not? Don't the philosophers and other gynæ-

72

cologists tell us that women will strike back with
any weapon, even their children?

STEVENS
(watching the child)
Including the sleeping pill you told me you gave
Gowan?

TEMPLE
All right.
(approaches table)
If I would just stop struggling: how much time
we could save. I came all the way back from California, but I still can't seem to quit. Do you believe
in coincidence?

STEVENS
(turns)
Not unless I have to.

TEMPLE
(at table, takes up a folded yellow tele-
graph form, opens it, reads)
Dated Jefferson, March sixth. 'You have a week
yet until the thirteenth. But where will you go
then?' signed Gavin.

She folds the paper back into its old creases, folds it still
again. Stevens watches her.

STEVENS
Well? This is the eleventh. Is that the coincidence?

TEMPLE
No. This is.
(she drops, tosses the folded paper onto
the table, turns)

c*

It was that afternoon—the sixth. We were on the
beach, Bucky and I. I was reading, and he was—
oh, talking mostly, you know—'Is California far
from Jefferson, mamma?' and I say 'Yes, darling'
—you know: still reading or trying to, and he
says, 'How long will we stay in California,
mamma?' and I say, 'Until we get tired of it' and
he says, 'Will we stay here until they hang Nancy,
mamma?' and it's already too late then; I should
have seen it coming but it's too late now; I say,
'Yes, darling' and then he drops it right in my lap,
right out of the mouths of—how is it?—babes and
sucklings. 'Where will we go then, mamma?' And
then we come back to the hotel, and there you are
too. Well?

STEVENS

Well what?

TEMPLE

All right. Let's for God's sake stop.
(goes to a chair)
Now that I'm here, no matter whose fault it was,
what do you want? A drink? Will you drink? At
least, put your coat and hat down.

STEVENS

I don't even know yet. That's why you came
back—

TEMPLE

(interrupts)
I came back? It wasn't I who——

STEVENS
(interrupts)
—who said, let's for God's sake stop.
They stare at each other: a moment.

TEMPLE
All right. Put down your coat and hat.
Stevens lays his hat and coat on a chair. Temple sits down.
Stevens takes a chair opposite, so that the sleeping child
on the sofa is between them in background.

So Nancy must be saved. So you send for me, or
you and Bucky between you, or anyway here you
are and here I am. Because apparently I know
something I haven't told yet, or maybe you
know something I haven't told yet. What do you
think you know?
(quickly; he says nothing)
All right. What do you know?

STEVENS
Nothing. I don't want to know it. All I——

TEMPLE
Say that again.

STEVENS
Say what again?

TEMPLE
What is it you think you know?

STEVENS
Nothing. I——

TEMPLE
All right. Why do you think there is something I
haven't told yet?

STEVENS

You came back. All the way from California——

TEMPLE

Not enough. Try again.

STEVENS

You were there.
> (with her face averted, Temple reaches
> her hand to the table, fumbles until she
> finds the cigarette box, takes a cigarette and
> with the same hand fumbles until she finds
> the lighter, draws them back to her lap)

At the trial. Every day. All day, from the time
court opened——

TEMPLE

> (still not looking at him, supremely
> casual, puts the cigarette into her mouth,
> talking around it, the cigarette bobbing)

The bereaved mother——

STEVENS

Yes, the bereaved mother——

TEMPLE

> (the cigarette bobbing: still not looking
> at him)

—herself watching the accomplishment of her
revenge; the tigress over the body of her slain
cub——

STEVENS

—who should have been too immersed in grief to
have thought of revenge—to have borne the very
sight of her child's murderer . . .

                    TEMPLE
              (not looking at him)
        Methinks she doth protest too much?
Stevens doesn't answer. She snaps the lighter on, lights
the cigarette, puts the lighter back on the table. Leaning,
Stevens pushes the ashtray along the table until she can
reach it. Now she looks at him.

                    TEMPLE
Thanks. Now let grandmamma teach you how to
suck an egg. It doesn't matter what I know, what
you think I know, what might have happened.
Because we won't even need it. All we need is an
affidavit. That she is crazy. Has been for years.

                    STEVENS
I thought of that too. Only it's too late. That
should have been done about five months ago.
The trial is over now. She has been convicted and
sentenced. In the eyes of the law, she is already
dead. In the eyes of the law, Nancy Mannigoe
doesn't even exist. Even if there wasn't a better
reason than that. The best reason of all.

                    TEMPLE
                  (smoking)
Yes?

                    STEVENS
We haven't got one.

                    TEMPLE
                  (smoking)
Yes?
                  (she sits back in the chair, smoking

> rapidly, looking at Stevens. Her voice is
> gentle, patient, only a little too rapid, like
> the smoking)

That's right. Try to listen. Really try. I am the
affidavit; what else are we doing here at ten o'clock
at night barely a day from her execution? What
else did I—as you put it—come all the way back
from California for, not to mention a—as you
have probably put that too—faked coincidence to
save—as I would put it I suppose—my face? All
we need now is to decide just how much of what
to put in the affidavit. Do try; maybe you had
better have a drink after all.

STEVENS
Later, maybe. I'm dizzy enough right now with
just perjury and contempt of court.

TEMPLE
What perjury?

STEVENS
Not venal then, worse: inept. After my client is
not only convicted but sentenced, I turn up with
the prosecution's chief witness offering evidence
to set the whole trial aside—

TEMPLE
Tell them I forgot this. Or tell them I changed my
mind. Tell them the district attorney bribed me
to keep my mouth shut——

STEVENS
> (peremptory yet quiet)

Temple.

She puffs rapidly at the cigarette, removes it from her mouth.

TEMPLE

Or better still; won't it be obvious? a woman whose child was smothered in its crib, wanting vengeance, capable of anything to get the vengeance; then when she has it, realising she can't go through with it, can't sacrifice a human life for it, even a nigger whore's?

STEVENS

Stop it. One at a time. At least, let's talk about the same thing.

TEMPLE

What else are we talking about except saving a condemned client whose trained lawyer has already admitted that he has failed?

STEVENS

Then you really don't want her to die. You did invent the coincidence.

TEMPLE

Didn't I just say so? At least, let's for God's sake stop that, can't we?

STEVENS

Done. So Temple Drake will have to save her.

TEMPLE

Mrs. Gowan Stevens will.

STEVENS

Temple Drake.

She stares at him, smoking, deliberately now. Deliber-

ately she removes the cigarette and, still watching him,
reaches and snubs it out in the ashtray.

> All right. Tell me again. Maybe I'll even under-
> stand this time, let alone listen. We produce—turn
> up with—a sworn affidavit that this murderess
> was crazy when she committed the crime.

TEMPLE

You did listen, didn't you? Who knows——

STEVENS

Based on what?

TEMPLE

—What?

STEVENS

The affidavit. Based on what?
> (she stares at him)
On what proof?

TEMPLE

Proof?

STEVENS

Proof. What will be in the affidavit? What are
we going to affirm now that for some reason, any
reason, we—you—we didn't see fit to bring up
or anyway didn't bring up until after she——

TEMPLE

How do I know? You're the lawyer. What do you
want in it? What do such affidavits have in them,
need to have in them, to make them work, make
them sure to work? Don't you have samples in
your law books—reports, whatever you call them

—that you can copy and have me swear to? Good ones, certain ones? At least, while we're committing whatever this is, pick out a good one, such a good one that nobody, not even an untrained lawyer, can punch holes in it. . . .

Her voice ceases. She stares at him, while he continues to look steadily back at her, saying nothing, just looking at her, until at last she draws a loud harsh breath; her voice is harsh too.

What do you want then? What more do you want?

STEVENS

Temple Drake.

TEMPLE
(quick, harsh, immediate)
No. Mrs. Gowan Stevens.

STEVENS
(implacable and calm)
Temple Drake. The truth.

TEMPLE

Truth? We're trying to save a condemned murderess whose lawyer has already admitted that he has failed. What has truth got to do with that?
(rapid, harsh)
We? I, *I,* the mother of the baby she murdered; not you, Gavin Stevens, the lawyer, but I, Mrs. Gowan Stevens, the mother. Can't you get it through your head that I will do anything, *any-thing?*

F

STEVENS

Except one. Which is all. We're not concerned
with death. That's nothing: any handful of petty
facts and sworn documents can cope with that.
That's all finished now; we can forget it. What
we are trying to deal with now is injustice. Only
truth can cope with that. Or love.

TEMPLE
(harshly)
Love. Oh, God. Love.

STEVENS

Call it pity then. Or courage. Or simple honour,
honesty, or a simple desire for the right to sleep
at night.

TEMPLE

You prate of sleep, to me, who learned six years
ago how not even to realise any more that I didn't
mind not sleeping at night?

STEVENS

Yet you invented the coincidence.

TEMPLE

Will you for Christ's sake stop? Will you . . . All
right. Then if her dying is nothing, what do you
want? What in God's name do you want?

STEVENS

I told you. Truth.

TEMPLE

And I told you that what you keep on harping at
as truth has nothing to do with this. When you go

before the—— What do you call this next collec-
tion of trained lawyers? supreme court?—what you
will need will be facts, papers, documents, sworn
to, incontrovertible, that no other lawyer trained
or untrained either can punch holes in, find any
flaw in.

STEVENS
We're not going to the supreme court.
                    (she stares at him)
That's all finished. If that could have been done,
would have sufficed, I would have thought of that,
attended to that, four months ago. We're going
to the Governor. Tonight.

TEMPLE
The Governor?

STEVENS
Perhaps he won't save her either. He probably
won't.

TEMPLE
Then why ask him? Why?

STEVENS
I've told you. Truth.

TEMPLE
                    (in quiet amazement)
For no more than that. For no better reason than
that. Just to get it told, breathed aloud, into words,
sound. Just to be heard by, told to, someone, anyone, any stranger none of whose business it is,
can possibly be, simply because he is capable of

hearing, comprehending it. Why blink your own
rhetoric? Why don't you go on and tell me it's
for the good of my soul—if I have one?

STEVENS

I did. I said, so you can sleep at night.

TEMPLE

And I told you I forgot six years ago even what
it was to miss the sleep.

She stares at him. He doesn't answer, looking at her.
Still watching him, she reaches her hand to the table,
toward the cigarette box, then stops, is motionless, her
hand suspended, staring at him.

There is something else, then. We're even going
to get the true one this time. All right. Shoot.

He doesn't answer, makes no sign, watching her. A moment, then she turns her head and looks toward the sofa
and the sleeping child. Still looking at the child, she rises
and crosses to the sofa and stands looking down at the
child; her voice is quiet.

So it was a plant, after all; I just didn't seem to
know for who.
(she looks down at the child)
I threw my remaining child at you. Now you
threw him back.

STEVENS

But I didn't wake him.

TEMPLE

Then I've got you, lawyer. What would be better
for his peace and sleep than to hang his sister's
murderer?

STEVENS

No matter by what means, in what lie?

TEMPLE

Nor whose.

STEVENS

Yet you invented the coincidence.

TEMPLE

Mrs. Gowan Stevens did.

STEVENS

Temple Drake did. Mrs. Gowan Stevens is not even fighting in this class. This is Temple Drake's.

TEMPLE

Temple Drake is dead.

STEVENS

The past is never dead. It's not even past.

She comes back to the table, takes a cigarette from the box, puts it in her mouth and reaches for the lighter. He leans as though to hand it to her, but she has already found it, snaps it on and lights the cigarette, talking through the smoke.

TEMPLE

Listen. How much do you know?

STEVENS

Nothing.

TEMPLE

Swear.

STEVENS

Would you believe me?

TEMPLE

No. But swear anyway.

STEVENS

All right. I swear.

TEMPLE

(crushes cigarette into tray)

Then listen. Listen carefully.

(she stands, tense, rigid, facing him,
staring at him)

Temple Drake is dead. Temple Drake will have
been dead six years longer than Nancy Mannigoe
will ever be. If all Nancy Mannigoe has to save her
is Temple Drake, then God help Nancy Mannigoe.
Now get out of here.

She stares at him; another moment. Then he rises, still
watching her; she stares steadily and implacably back.
Then he moves.

Good night.

STEVENS

Good night.

He goes back to the chair, takes up his coat and hat, then
goes on to the hall door, has put his hand on the knob.

TEMPLE

Gavin.

(he pauses, his hand on the knob, and
looks back at her)

Maybe I'll have the handkerchief, after all.

(he looks at her a moment longer, then
releases the knob, takes the handkerchief
from his breast pocket as he crosses

back toward her, extends it. She doesn't
take it)
All right. What will I have to do? What do you
suggest, then?

STEVENS
Everything.

TEMPLE
Which of course I won't. I will not. You can
understand that, can't you? At least you can hear
it. So let's start over, shall we? How much will I
have to tell?

STEVENS
Everything.

TEMPLE
Then I won't need the handkerchief, after all.
Good night. Close the front door when you go
out, please. It's getting cold again.

He turns, crosses again to the door without stopping nor
looking back, exits, closes the door behind him. She is
not watching him either now. For a moment after the
door has closed, she doesn't move. Then she makes a gesture something like Gowan's in Scene Two, except that
she merely presses her palms for a moment hard against
her face, her face calm, expressionless, cold, drops her
hands, turns, picks up the crushed cigarette from beside
the tray and puts it into the tray and takes up the tray
and crosses to the fireplace, glancing down at the sleeping
child as she passes the sofa, empties the tray into the fireplace and returns to the table and puts the tray on it and
this time pauses at the sofa and stoops and tucks the

blanket closer about the sleeping child and then goes on
to the telephone and lifts the receiver.
                    (into the phone)
    Three-two-nine, please.
                            (while she stands waiting for the answer,
                            there is a slight movement in the darkness
                            beyond the open door at rear, just enough
                            silent movement to show that something
                            or someone is there or has moved there.
                            Temple is unaware of it since her back
                            is turned. Then she speaks into the phone)
    Maggie? Temple. . . . Yes, suddenly . . . Oh, I
    don't know; perhaps we got bored with sunshine.
    . . . Of course, I may drop in tomorrow. I wanted
    to leave a message for Gavin . . . I know; he's just
    left here. Something I forgot . . . If you'll ask him
    to call me when he comes in. . . . Yes. . . .Wasn't
    it. . . . Yes. . . . If you will . . . Thank you.
                            (she puts the receiver down and starts to
                            turn back into the room when the tele-
                            phone rings. She turns back, takes up the
                            receiver, speaks into it)
    Hello . . . Yes. Coincidence again; I had my hand
    on it; I had just called Maggie. . . . Oh, the filling
    station. I didn't think you had had time. I can be
    ready in thirty minutes. Your car, or ours? . . . All
    right. Listen. . . . Yes, I'm here. Gavin . . . How
    much will I have to tell?
                    (hurriedly)
    Oh, I know: you've already told me eight or ten
    times. But maybe I didn't here it right. How much
    will I have to tell?

> (she listens a moment, quiet, frozen-
> faced, then slowly begins to lower the
> receiver toward the stand; she speaks
> quietly, without inflection)

Oh, God. Oh, God.

She puts the receiver down, crosses to the sofa, snaps off
the table lamp and takes up the child and crosses to the
door to the hall, snaps off the remaining room lights as
she goes out, so that the only light in the room now enters
from the hall. As soon as she has disappeared from sight,
Gowan enters from the door at rear, dressed except for
his coat, waistcoat and tie. He has obviously taken no
sleeping pill. He goes to the phone and stands quietly
beside it, facing the hall door and obviously listening
until Temple is safely away. Now the hall light snaps off,
and the stage is in complete darkness.

GOWAN'S VOICE
> (quietly)

Three-two-nine, please . . . Good evening, Aunt
Maggie. Gowan . . . All right, thank you . . .
Sure, some time tomorrow. As soon as Uncle
Gavin comes in, will you have him call me? I'll
be right here. Thank you.

Sound of the receiver as he puts it back.

(CURTAIN)

ACT TWO

THE GOLDEN DOME (Beginning Was the Word)

JACKSON. Alt. 294 ft. Pop. (A.D. 1950) 201,092.

Located by an expedition of three Commissioners selected appointed and dispatched for that single purpose, on a high bluff above Pearl River at the approximate geographical centre of the State, to be not a market nor industrial town, nor even as a place for men to live, but to be a capital, the Capital of a Commonwealth;

In the beginning was already decreed this rounded knob, this gilded pustule, already before and beyond the steamy chiaroscuro, untimed unseasoned winterless miasma not any one of water or earth or life yet all of each, inextricable and indivisible; that one seethe one spawn one mother-womb, one furious tumescence, father-mother-one, one vast incubant ejaculation already fissionating in one boiling moil of litter from the celestial experimental Work Bench; that one spawning crawl and creep printing with three-toed mastodonic tracks the steamy-green swaddling clothes of the coal and the oil, above which the pea-brained reptilian heads curved the heavy leather-flapped air;

Then the ice, but still this knob, this pimple-dome, this buried half-ball hemisphere; the earth lurched, heaving darkward the long continental flank, dragging upward beneath the polar cap that furious equatorial womb, the shutter-lid of cold severing off into blank and heedless

void one last sound, one cry, one puny myriad indictment
already fading and then no more, the blind and tongue-
less earth spinning on, looping the long recordless astral
orbit, frozen, tideless, yet still was there this tiny gleam,
this spark, this gilded crumb of man's eternal aspiration,
this golden dome preordained and impregnable, this
minuscule fœtus-glint tougher than ice and harder than
freeze; the earth lurched again, sloughing; the ice with
infinitesimal speed, scouring out the valleys, scoring the
hills, and vanished; the earth tilted further to recede the
sea rim by necklace-rim of crustacean husks in recessional
contour lines like the concentric whorls within the sawn
stump telling the tree's age, bearing south by recessional
south toward that mute and beckoning gleam the conflu-
ent continental swale, baring to light and air the broad
blank mid-continental page for the first scratch of orderly
recording—a laboratory-factory covering what would be
twenty states, established and ordained for the purpose of
manufacturing one: the ordered unhurried whirl of sea-
sons, of rain and snow and freeze and thaw and sun and
drouth to aerate and slack the soil, the conflux of a hundred rivers into one vast father of rivers carrying the rich
dirt, the rich garnering, south and south, carving the bluffs
to bear the long march of the river towns, flooding the
Mississippi lowlands, spawning the rich alluvial dirt layer
by vernal layer, raising inch by foot by year by century
the surface of the earth which in time (not distant now,
measured against that long signatureless chronicle) would
tremble to the passing of trains like when the cat crosses
the suspension bridge;

The rich deep black alluvial soil which would grow cot-

ton taller than the head of a man on a horse, already one
jungle one brake one impassable density of brier and cane
and vine interlocking the soar of gum and cypress and
hickory and pinoak and ash, printed now by the tracks
of unalien shapes—bear and deer and panthers and bison
and wolves and alligators and the myriad smaller beasts,
and unalien men to name them too perhaps—the (themselves) nameless though recorded predecessors who built
the mounds to escape the spring floods and left their
meagre artifacts: the obsolete and the dispossessed, dispossessed by those who were dispossessed in turn because
they too were obsolete: the wild Algonquian, Chickasaw
and Choctaw and Natchez and Pascagoula, peering in
virgin astonishment down from the tall bluffs at a Chip-
peway canoe bearing three Frenchmen—and had barely
time to whirl and look behind him at ten and then a
hundred and then a thousand Spaniards come overland
from the Atlantic Ocean: a tide, a wash, a thrice flux-and-
ebb of motion so rapid and quick across the land's slow
alluvial chronicle as to resemble the limber flicking of
the magician's one hand before the other holding the deck
of inconstant cards: the Frenchman for a moment, then
the Spaniard for perhaps two, then the Frenchman for
another two and then the Spaniard again for another and
then the Frenchman for that one last second, half-breath;
because then came the Anglo-Saxon, the pioneer, the
tall man, roaring with Protestant scripture and boiled
whiskey, Bible and jug in one hand and (like as not) a
native tomahawk in the other, brawling, turbulent not
through viciousness but simply because of his over-revved
glands; uxorious and polygamous: a married invincible
bachelor, dragging his gravid wife and most of the rest

of his mother-in-law's family behind him into the trackless infested forest, spawning that child as like as not
behind the barricade of a rifle-crotched log mapless
leagues from nowhere and then getting her with another
one before reaching his final itch-footed destination, and
at the same time scattering his ebullient seed in a hundred
dusky bellies through a thousand miles of wilderness;
innocent and gullible, without bowels for avarice or
compassion or forethought either, changing the face of
the earth: felling a tree which took two hundred years to
grow, in order to extract from it a bear or a capful of
wild honey;

Obsolete too: still felling the two-hundred-year-old tree
when the bear and the wild honey were gone and there
was nothing in it any more but a raccoon or a possum
whose hide was worth at the most two dollars, turning the
earth into a howling waste from which he would be the
first to vanish, not even on the heels but synchronous
with the slightly darker wild men whom he had dispossessed, because, like them, only the wilderness could feed
and nourish him; and so disappeared, strutted his roaring
eupeptic hour, and was no more, leaving his ghost, pariah
and proscribed, scriptureless now and armed only with
the highwayman's, the murderer's, pistol, haunting the
fringes of the wilderness which he himself had helped to
destroy, because the river towns marched now recessional
south by south along the processional bluffs: St. Louis,
Paducah, Memphis, Helena, Vicksburg, Natchez, Baton
Rouge, peopled by men with mouths full of law, in
broadcloth and flowered waistcoats, who owned Negro
slaves and Empire beds and buhl cabinets and ormolu

clocks, who strolled and smoked their cigars along the bluffs beneath which in the shanty and flatboat purlieus he rioted out the last of his doomed evening, losing his worthless life again and again to the fierce knives of his drunken and worthless kind—this in the intervals of being pursued and harried in his vanishing avatars of Harpe and Hare and Mason and Murrel, either shot on sight or hoicked, dragged out of what remained of his secret wilderness haunts along the overland Natchez trace (one day someone brought a curious seed into the land and inserted it into the earth, and now vast fields of white not only covered the waste places which with his wanton and heedless axe he had made, but were effacing, thrusting back the wilderness even faster than he had been able to, so that he barely had a screen for his back when, crouched in his thicket, he glared at his dispossessor in impotent and incredulous and uncomprehending rage) into the towns to his formal apotheosis in a courtroom and then a gallows or the limb of a tree;

Because those days were gone, the old brave innocent tumultuous eupeptic tomorrowless days; the last broadhorn and keelboat (Mike Fink was a legend; soon even the grandfathers would no longer claim to remember him, and the river hero was now the steamboat gambler wading ashore in his draggled finery from the towhead where the captain had marooned him) had been sold piecemeal for firewood in Chartres and Toulouse and Dauphine Street, and Choctaw and Chickasaw braves, in short hair and overalls and armed with mule-whips in place of warclubs and already packed up to move west to Oklahoma, watched steamboats furrowing even the shallowest and

remotest wilderness streams where tumbled gently to the
motion of the paddle-wheels, the gutted rock-weighted
bones of Hare's and Mason's murderees; a new time, a
new age, millennium's beginning; one vast single net of
commerce webbed and veined the mid-continent's fluvial
embracement; New Orleans, Pittsburgh, and Fort Brid-
ger, Wyoming, were suburbs one to the other, inextricable in destiny; men's mouths were full of law and order,
all men's mouths were round with the sound of money;
one unanimous golden affirmation ululated the nation's
boundless immeasurable forenoon: profit plus regimen
equals security: a nation of commonwealths; that crumb,
that dome, that gilded pustule, that Idea risen now, suspended like a balloon or a portent or a thundercloud above
what used to be wilderness, drawing, holding the eyes of
all: Mississippi: a state, a commonwealth; triumvirate in
legislative, judiciary, executive, but without a capital,
functioning as though from a field headquarters, operat-
ing as though still *en route* toward that high inevitable
place in the galaxy of commonwealths, so in 1820 from
its field p.c. at Columbia the legislature selected appointed
and dispatched the three Commissioners Hinds, Lattimore
and Patton, not three politicians and less than any three
political time-servers but soldiers engineers and patriots—
soldier to cope with the reality, engineer to cope with the
aspiration, patriot to hold fast to the dream—three white
men in a Choctaw pirogue moving slowly up the empty
reaches of a wilderness river as two centuries ago the
three Frenchmen had drifted in their Northern birchbark
down that vaster and emptier one;

But not drifting, these: paddling: because this was upstream, bearing not volitionless into the unknown mystery and authority, but establishing in the wilderness a point for men to rally to in conscience and free will, scanning, watching the dense inscrutable banks in their turn too, conscious of the alien incorrigible eyes too perhaps but already rejectant of them, not that the wilderness's dark denizens, already dispossessed at Doak's Stand, were less inveterate now, but because this canoe bore not the meek and bloody cross of Christ and Saint Louis, but the scales the blindfold and the sword—up the river to Le Fleur's Bluff, the trading-post store on the high mild promontory established by the Canadian *voyageur*, whose name, called and spelled 'Leflore' now, would be borne by the half-French half-Choctaw hereditary first chief of the Choctaw nation who, siding with the white men at the Council of Dancing Rabbit, would remain in Mississippi after his people departed for the west, to become in time among the first of the great slave-holding cotton planters and leave behind him a county and its seat named for himself and a plantation named in honour of a French king's mistress—stopping at last though still paddling slowly to hold the pirogue against the current, looking not up at the dark dispossessed faces watching them from the top of the bluff, but looking staring rather from one to another among themselves in the transfixed boat, saying, 'This is the city. This is the State';

1821, General Hinds and his co-commissioners, with Abraham DeFrance, superintendent of public buildings at Washington, to advise them, laid out the city according to Thomas Jefferson's plan to Territorial Governor Claiborne seventeen years ago, and built the statehouse,

thirty by forty feet of brick and clay and native limestone
yet large enough to contain the dream; the first legislature convened in it in the new year 1822;

And named the city after the other old hero, hero Hinds'
brother-in-arms on beaten British and Seminole fields
and presently to be President—the old duellist, the brawling lean fierce mangy durable old lion who set the well-
being of the Nation above the White House, and the
health of his new political party above either, and above
them all set, not his wife's honour, but the principle that
honour must be defended whether it was or not since,
defended, it was, whether or not;—Jackson, that the new
city created not for a city but a central point for the
governance of men, might partake of the successful soldier's courage and endurance and luck, and named the
area surrounding it 'Hinds County' after the lesser hero,
as the hero's quarters, even empty, not only partake of
his dignity but even guard and increase its stature;

And needed them, the luck at least: in 1829 the Senate
passed a bill authorising the removal of the capital to
Clinton, the House defeated it; in 1830 the House itself
voted to move to Port Gibson on the Mississippi, but
with the next breath reconsidered, renegued, the following
day they voted to move to Vicksburg but nothing came of
that either, no records (Sherman burned them in 1863
and notified his superior, General Grant, by note of hand
with comfortable and encouraging brevity) to show just
what happened this time: a trial, a dry run perhaps or
perhaps still enchannelled by a week's or a month's rut
of habit or perhaps innocent in juvenility, absent or any-

way missing the unanimous voice or presence of the three patriot-dreamers who forced the current and bore the dream, like a child with dynamite: innocent of its own power for alteration: until in 1832, perhaps in simple self-defence or perhaps in simple weariness, a constitution was written designating Jackson as the capital if not in perpetuity at least in escrow until 1850, when (hoped perhaps) a maturer legislature would be composed of maturer men outgrown or anyway become used to the novelty of manipulation;

Which by that time was enough; Jackson was secure, impregnable to simple toyment; fixed and founded strong, it would endure always; men had come there to live and the railroads had followed them, crossing off with steel cancellations the age of the steamboat: in '36 to Vicksburg, in '37 to Natchez, then last of all the junction of two giving a route from New Orleans to Tennessee and the Southern railroad to New York and the Atlantic Ocean; secure and fixed: in 1836 Old Hickory himself addressed the legislature in its own halls, five years later Henry Clay was entertained under that roof; it knew the convention called to consider Clay's last compromise, it saw that Convention in 1861 which declared Mississippi to be the third star in that new galaxy of commonwealth dedicated to the principle that voluntary communities of men shall be not just safe but even secured from Federal meddling, and knew General Pemberton while defending that principle and right, and Joseph Johnston: and Sherman: and fire: and nothing remained, a City of Chimneys (once pigs rooted in the streets; now rats did) ruled over by a general of the United States Army while the new blood poured in: men who had followed, pressed close the Federal field armies with spoiled grain and tainted meat and spavined mules, now pressing close the Federal provost-marshals with carpet bags stuffed with blank ballot-forms on which freed slaves could mark their formal X's;

But endured; the government, which fled before Sherman in 1863, returned in '65, and even grew too despite the fact that a city government of carpet-baggers held on long after the state as a whole had dispossessed them; in 1869 Tougaloo College for Negroes was founded, in 1884 Jackson College for Negroes was brought from Natchez, in 1898 Campbell College for Negroes removed from Vicksburg: Negro leaders developed by these schools intervened when in 1868 one 'Buzzard' Egglestone instigated the use of troops to drive Governor Humphries from the executive offices and mansion; in 1887 Jackson women sponsored the Kermis Ball lasting three days to raise money for a monument to the Confederate dead; in 1844 Jefferson Davis spoke for his last time in public at the old Capitol; in 1890 the state's greatest convention drew up the present constitution;

And still the people and the railroads: the New Orleans and Great Northern down the Pearl River valley, the Gulf Mobile and Northern north-east; Alabama and the eastern black prairies were almost a commuter's leap and a line to Yazoo City and the upper river towns made of the Great Lakes five suburban ponds; the Gulf and Ship Island opened the south Mississippi lumber boom and Chicago voices spoke among the magnolias and the odour of jasmine and oleander; population doubled and trebled in a decade, in 1892 Millsaps College opened its doors to assume its place among the first establishments for higher learning; then the natural gas and the oil, Texas and Oklahoma licence plates flitted like a migration of birds about the land and the tall flames from the vent-pipes stood like incandescent plumes above the century-cold ashes of Choctaw camp-fires and the vanished imprints of deer; and in 1903 the new Capitol was completed— the golden dome, the knob, the gleamy crumb, the gilded pustule longer than the miasma and the gigantic ephemeral saurians, more durable than the ice and the prenight cold, soaring, hanging as one blinding spheroid above the centre of the Commonwealth, incapable of being either looked full or evaded, peremptory, irrefragable, and reassuring;

In the roster of Mississippi names:
Claiborne. Humphries. Dickson. McLaurin. Barksdale. Lamar. Prentiss. Davis. Sartoris. Compson;

In the roster of cities:
JACKSON. Alt. 294 ft. Pop. (A.D. 1950) 201,092.
Railroads: Illinois Central, Yazoo & Mississippi Valley, Alabama & Vicksburg, Gulf & Ship Island.
Bus: Tri-State Transit, Vanardo, Thomas, Greyhound, Dixie-Greyhound, Teche-Greyhound, Oliver.
Air: Delta, Chicago & Southern.
Transport: Street buses, Taxis.
Accommodations: Hotels, Tourist camps, Rooming houses.
Radio: WJDX, WTJS.

Diversions: chronic: S.I.A.A., Basketball Tournament, Music Festival, Junior Auxiliary Follies, May Day Festival, State Tennis Tournament, Red Cross Water Pageant, State Fair, Junior Auxiliary Style Show, Girl Scouts Horse Show, Feast of Carols.

Diversions: acute: Religion, Politics.

Office of the Governor of the State. 2.00 A.M. March
twelfth.

The whole bottom of the stage is in darkness, as in Scene
I, Act I, so that the visible scene has the effect of being
held in the beam of a spotlight. Suspended too, since it
is upper left and even higher above the shadow of the
stage proper than the same in Scene I, Act I, carrying still
further the symbolism of the still higher, the last, the
ultimate seat of judgment.

It is a corner or section of the office of the Governor of
the Commonwealth, late at night, about 2 A.M.—a clock
on the wall says two minutes past two—a massive flat-
topped desk bare except for an ashtray and a telephone,
behind it a high-backed heavy chair like a throne; on the
wall behind and above the chair, is the emblem, official
badge, of the state, sovereignty (a mythical one, since
this is rather the state of which Yoknapatawpha County
is a unit)—an eagle, the blind scales of justice, a device in
Latin perhaps, against a flag. There are two other chairs in
front of the desk, turned slightly to face each other, the
length of the desk between them.

The Governor stands in front of the high chair, between
it and the desk, beneath the emblem on the wall. He is
symbolic too: no known person, neither old nor young;
he might be someone's idea not of God but of Gabriel
perhaps, the Gabriel not before the Crucifixion but after
it. He has obviously just been routed out of bed or at

least out of his study or dressing-room; he wears a
dressing-gown, though there is a collar and tie beneath
it, and his hair is neatly combed.

Temple and Stevens have just entered. Temple wears the
same fur coat, hat, bag, gloves, etc., as in Scene II, Act I,
Stevens is dressed exactly as he was in Scene III, Act I,
is carrying his hat. They are moving toward the two
chairs at either end of the desk.

                    STEVENS
          Good morning, Henry. Here we are.

                    GOVERNOR
          Yes. Sit down.
                    (as Temple sits down)
          Does Mrs. Stevens smoke?

                    STEVENS
          Yes. Thank you.
He takes a pack of cigarettes from his topcoat pocket, as
though he had come prepared for the need, emergency.
He works one of them free and extends the pack to
Temple. The Governor puts one hand into his dressing-
gown pocket and withdraws it, holding something in his
closed fist.

                    TEMPLE
                    (takes the cigarette)
          What, no blindfold?
                         (the Governor extends his hand across the
                         desk. It contains a lighter. Temple puts
                         the cigarette into her mouth. The Gover-
                         nor snaps on the lighter)

But of course, the only one waiting execution is back there in Jefferson. So all we need to do here is fire away, and hope that at least the volley rids us of the metaphor.

GOVERNOR

Metaphor?

TEMPLE

The blindfold. The firing squad. Or is metaphor wrong? Or maybe it's the joke. But don't apologise; a joke that has to be diagrammed is like trying to excuse an egg, isn't it? The only thing you can do is, bury them both, quick.

> (the Governor approaches the flame to Temple's cigarette. She leans and accepts the light, then sits back)

Thanks.

The Governor closes the lighter, sits down in the tall chair behind the desk, still holding the lighter in his hand, his hands resting on the desk before him. Stevens sits down in the other chair across from Temple, laying the pack of cigarettes on the desk beside him.

GOVERNOR

What has Mrs. Gowan Stevens to tell me?

TEMPLE

Not tell you: ask you. No, that's wrong. I could have asked you to revoke or commute or whatever you do to a sentence to hang when we— Uncle Gavin telephoned you last night.

> (to Stevens)

Go on. Tell him. Aren't you the mouthpiece?—

D*

isn't that how you say it? Don't lawyers always tell their patients—I mean clients—never to say anything at all: to let them do all the talking?

GOVERNOR

That's only before the client enters the witness stand.

TEMPLE

So this is the witness stand.

GOVERNOR

You have come all the way here from Jefferson at two o'clock in the morning. What would you call it?

TEMPLE

All right. *Touché* then. But not Mrs. Gowan Stevens: Temple Drake. You remember Temple: the all-Mississippi debutante whose finishing school was the Memphis sporting house? About eight years ago, remember? Not that anyone, certainly not the sovereign state of Mississippi's first paid servant, need be reminded of that, provided they could read newspapers eight years ago or were kin to somebody who could read eight years ago or even had a friend who could or even just hear or even just remember or just believe the worst or even just hope for it.

GOVERNOR

I think I remember. What has Temple Drake to tell me then?

TEMPLE

That's not first. The first thing is, how much will

I have to tell? I mean, how much of it that you don't already know, so that I won't be wasting all of our times telling it over? It's two o'clock in the morning; you want to—maybe even need to—sleep some, even if you are our first paid servant; maybe even because of that—— You see? I'm already lying. What does it matter to me how much sleep the state's first paid servant loses, any more than it matters to the first paid servant, a part of whose job is being paid to lose sleep over the Nancy Mannigoes and Temple Drakes?

STEVENS
Not lying.

TEMPLE
All right. Stalling, then. So maybe if his excellency or his honour or whatever they call him, will answer the question, we can get on.

STEVENS
Why not let the question go, and just get on?

GOVERNOR
(to Temple)
Ask me your question. How much of what do I already know?

TEMPLE
(after a moment: she doesn't answer at
first, staring at the Governor: then:)
Uncle Gavin's right. Maybe you are the one to ask the questions. Only, make it as painless as possible. Because it's going to be a little . . . painful, to put it euphoniously—at least 'euphonious'

is right, isn't it?—no matter who bragged about
blindfolds.

GOVERNOR

Tell me about Nancy—Mannihoe, Mannikoe—
how does she spell it?

TEMPLE

She doesn't. She can't. She can't read or write
either. You are hanging her under Mannigoe,
which may be wrong too, though after tomorrow
morning it won't matter.

GOVERNOR

Oh yes, Manigault. The old Charleston name.

STEVENS

Older than that. Maingault. Nancy's heritage—
or anyway her patronym—runs Norman blood.

GOVERNOR

Why not start by telling me about her?

TEMPLE

You are so wise. She was a dope-fiend whore that
my husband and I took out of the gutter to nurse
our children. She murdered one of them and is to
be hung tomorrow morning. We—her lawyer and
I—have come to ask you to save her.

GOVERNOR

Yes. I know all that. Why?

TEMPLE

Why am I, the mother whose child she murdered,
asking you to save her? Because I have forgiven her.

(the Governor watches her, he and
Stevens both do, waiting. She stares back
at the Governor steadily, not defiant:
just alert)

Because she was crazy.

(the Governor watches her: she stares
back, puffing rapidly at the cigarette)

All right. You don't mean why I am asking you
to save her, but why I—we hired a whore and a
tramp and a dope-fiend to nurse our children.

(she puffs rapidly, talking through the
smoke)

To give her another chance—a human being too,
even a nigger dope-fiend whore——

STEVENS

Nor that, either.

TEMPLE

(rapidly, with a sort of despair)

Oh yes, not even stalling now. Why can't you
stop lying? You know: just stop for a while or a
time like you can stop playing tennis or running
or dancing or drinking or eating sweets during
Lent. You know: not to reform: just to quit for
a while, clear your system, rest up for a new tune
or set or lie? All right. It was to have someone to
talk to. And now you see? I'll have to tell the rest
of it in order to tell you why I had to have a dope-
fiend whore to talk to, why Temple Drake, the
white woman, the all-Mississippi debutante, descendant of long lines of statesmen and soldiers high
and proud in the high proud annals of our sovereign

state, couldn't find anybody except a nigger dope-
fiend whore that could speak her language——

GOVERNOR

Yes. This far, this late at night. Tell it.

TEMPLE

(she puffs rapidly at the cigarette, leans
and crushes it out in the ashtray and sits
erect again. She speaks in a hard rapid
brittle emotionless voice)

Whore, dope-fiend; hopeless, already damned
before she was ever born, whose only reason for
living was to get the chance to die a murderess
on the gallows.—Who not only entered the home
of the socialite Gowan Stevenses out of the gutter,
but made her debut into the public life of her
native city while lying in the gutter with a white
man trying to kick her teeth or at least her voice
back down her throat.—You remember, Gavin:
what was his name? it was before my time in
Jefferson, but you remember: the cashier in the
bank, the pillar of the church or anyway in the
name of his childless wife; and this Monday morning and still drunk, Nancy comes up while he is
unlocking the front door of the bank and fifty
people standing at his back to get in, and Nancy
comes into the crowd and right up to him and
says, 'Where's my two dollars, white man?' and
he turned and struck her, knocked her across the
pavement into the gutter and then ran after her,
stomping and kicking at her face or anyway her
voice which was still saying 'Where's my two

dollars, white man?' until the crowd caught and held him still kicking at the face lying in the gutter, spitting blood and teeth and still saying, 'It was two dollars more than two weeks ago and you done been back twice since'——

She stops speaking, presses both hands to her face for an instant, then removes them.

No, no handkerchief; Lawyer Stevens and I made a dry run on handkerchiefs before we left home tonight. Where was I?

GOVERNOR
(quotes her)
'It was already two dollars'——

TEMPLE
So now I've got to tell all of it. Because that was just Nancy Mannigoe. Temple Drake was in more than just a two-dollar Saturday-night house. But then, I said *touché*, didn't I?

She leans forward and starts to take up the crushed cigarette from the ashtray. Stevens picks up the pack from the desk and prepares to offer it to her. She withdraws her hand from the crushed cigarette and sits back.

(to the proffered cigarette in Stevens' hand)

No, thanks; I won't need it, after all. From here out, it's merely anticlimax. *Coup de grâce.* The victim never feels that, does he?—Where was I?

(quickly)

Never mind. I said that before too, didn't I?

(she sits for a moment, her hands gripped in her lap, motionless)

There seems to be some of this, quite a lot of this, which even our first paid servant is not up on; maybe because he has been our first paid servant for less than two years yet. Though that's wrong too; he could read eight years ago, couldn't he? In fact, he couldn't have been elected Governor of even Mississippi if he hadn't been able to read at least three years in advance, could he?

STEVENS

Temple.

TEMPLE
(to Stevens)
Why not? It's just stalling, isn't it?

GOVERNOR
(watching Temple)
Hush, Gavin.
(to Temple)
Coup de grâce not only means mercy, but is. Deliver it. Give her the cigarette, Gavin.

TEMPLE
(sits forward again)
No, thanks. Really.
(after a second)
Sorry.
(quickly)
You'll notice, I always remember to say that, always remember my manners,—'raising' as we put it. Showing that I really sprang from gentle-folks, not Norman knights like Nancy did, but at least people who don't insult the host in his own

house, especially at two o'clock in the morning.
Only, I just sprang too far, where Nancy merely
stumbled modestly: a lady again, you see.

(after a moment)

There again. I'm not even stalling now: I'm fault-
ing—what do they call it? burking. You know:
here we are at the fence again; we've got to jump
it this time, or crash. You know: slack the snaffle,
let her mouth it a little, take hold, a light hold,
just enough to have something to jump against;
then touch her. So here we are, right back where
we started, and so we can start over. So how much
will I have to tell, say, speak out loud so that anybody with ears can hear it, about Temple Drake
that I never thought that anything on earth, least
of all the murder of my child and the execution of
a nigger dope-fiend whore, would ever make me
tell? That I came here at two o'clock in the morning to wake you up to listen to, after eight years of
being safe, or at least quiet? You know: how much
will I have to tell, to make it good and painful of
course, but quick too, so that you can revoke or
commute the sentence or whatever you do to it,
and we can all go back home to sleep or at least to
bed? Painful of course, but just painful enough—I
think you said 'euphoniously' was right, didn't you?

GOVERNOR

Death is painful. A shameful one, even more so
—which is not too euphonious, even at best.

TEMPLE

Oh, death. We're not talking about death now.

We're talking about shame. Nancy Mannigoe has
no shame; all she has is, to die. But *touché* for me
too; haven't I brought Temple Drake all the way
here at two o'clock in the morning for the reason
that all Nancy Mannigoe has, is to die?

STEVENS

Tell him, then.

TEMPLE

He hasn't answered my question yet.
(to Governor)
Try to answer it. How much will I have to tell?
Don't just say 'everything'. I've already heard
that.

GOVERNOR

I know who Temple Drake was: the young
woman student at the University eight years ago
who left the school one morning on a special train
of students to attend a baseball game at another
college, and disappeared from the train somewhere
during its run, and vanished, nobody knew where,
until she reappeared six weeks later as a witness in
a murder trial in Jefferson, produced by the lawyer
of the man who, it was then learned, had abducted
her and held her prisoner——

TEMPLE

—in the Memphis sporting house: don't forget
that.

GOVERNOR

—in order to produce her to prove his alibi in
the murder——

TEMPLE

—that Temple Drake knew had done the murder
for the very good reason that——

STEVENS

Wait. Let me play too. She got off the train at the
instigation of a young man who met the train at an
intermediate stop with an automobile, the plan
being to drive on to the ball game in the car,
except that the young man was drunk at the time
and got drunker, and wrecked the car and stranded
both of them at the moonshiner's house where the
murder happened, and from which the murderer
kidnapped her and carried her to Memphis, to hold
her until he would need his alibi. Afterward he—
the young man with the automobile, her escort and
protector at the moment of the abduction—married
her. He is her husband now. He is my nephew.

TEMPLE

(to Stevens, bitterly)

You too. So wise too. Why can't you believe in
truth? At least that I'm trying to tell it. At least
trying now to tell it.

(to Governor)

Where was I?

GOVERNOR

(quotes)

That Temple Drake knew had done the murder
for the very good reason that——

TEMPLE

Oh yes—for the very good reason that she saw

him do it, or at least his shadow: and so produced by his lawyer in the Jefferson courtroom so that she could swear away the life of the man who was accused of it. Oh yes, that's the one. And now I've already told you something you nor nobody else but the Memphis lawyer knew, and I haven't even started. You see? I can't even bargain with you. You haven't even said yes or no yet, whether you can save her or not, whether you want to save her or not, will consider saving her or not; which, if either of us, Temple Drake or Mrs. Gowan Stevens either, had any sense, would have demanded first of you.

GOVERNOR

Do you want to ask me that first?

TEMPLE

I can't. I don't dare. You might say no.

GOVERNOR

Then you wouldn't have to tell me about Temple Drake.

TEMPLE

I've got to do that. I've got to say it all, or I wouldn't be here. But unless I can still believe that you might say yes, I don't see how I can. Which is another *touché* for somebody: God, maybe—if there is one. You see? That's what's so terrible. We don't even need Him. Simple evil is enough. Even after eight years, it's still enough. It was eight years ago that Uncle Gavin said—oh yes, he was there too; didn't you just hear him? He could have told you all of this or anyway most of it over the telephone and you could be in bed asleep right this minute—said how there is a corruption even in just looking at evil, even by accident; that you can't haggle, traffic, with putrefaction—you can't, you don't dare—

(she stops, tense, motionless)

GOVERNOR

Take the cigarette now.

(to Stevens)

Gavin——

(Stevens takes up the pack and prepares to offer the cigarette)

TEMPLE

No, thanks. It's too late now. Because here we go. If we can't jump the fence, we can at least break through it——

STEVENS

(interrupts)

Which means that anyway one of us will get over standing up.

(as Temple reacts)

Oh yes, I'm still playing; I'm going to ride this one too. Go ahead.

(prompting)

Temple Drake——

TEMPLE

—Temple Drake, the foolish virgin; that is, a virgin as far as anybody went on record to disprove, but a fool certainly by anybody's standards

and computation; seventeen, and more of a fool
than simply being a virgin or even being seventeen
could excuse or account for; indeed, showing herself capable of a height of folly which even seven
or three, let alone mere virginity, could scarcely
have matched——

STEVENS

Give the brute a chance. Try at least to ride him
at the fence and not just through it.

TEMPLE

You mean the Virginia gentlemen.
    (to Governor)
That's my husband. He went to the University
of Virginia, trained, Uncle Gavin would say, at
Virginia not only in drinking but in gentility
too——

STEVENS

—and ran out of both at the same instant that day
eight years ago when he took her off the train
and wrecked the car at the moonshiner's house.

TEMPLE

But relapsed into one of them at least because at
least he married me as soon as he could.
    (to Stevens)
You don't mind my telling his excellency that, do
you?

STEVENS

A relapse into both of them. He hasn't had a drink
since that day either. His excellency might bear
that in mind too.

GOVERNOR

I will. I have.

> (he makes just enough of a pause to
> cause them both to stop and look at him)

I almost wish——

> (they are both watching him; this is the
> first intimation we have that something
> is going on here, an undercurrent: that
> the Governor and Stevens know some-
> thing which Temple doesn't: to Temple)

He didn't come with you.

STEVENS
> (mildly yet quickly)

Won't there be time for that later, Henry?

TEMPLE
> (quick, defiant, suspicious, hard)

Who didn't?

GOVERNOR

Your husband.

TEMPLE
> (quick and hard)

Why?

GOVERNOR

You have come here to plead for the life of the
murderess of your child. Your husband was its
parent too.

TEMPLE

You're wrong. We didn't come here at two
o'clock in the morning to save Nancy Mannigoe.

Nancy Mannigoe is not even concerned in this because Nancy Mannigoe's lawyer told me before we ever left Jefferson that you were not going to save Nancy Mannigoe. What we came here and waked you up at two o'clock in the morning for is just to give Temple Drake a good fair honest chance to suffer—you know: just anguish for the sake of anguish, like that Russian or somebody who wrote a whole book about suffering, not suffering for or about anything, just suffering, like somebody unconscious not really breathing for anything but just breathing. Or maybe that's wrong too and nobody really cares, suffers, any more about suffering than they do about truth or justice or Temple Drake's shame or Nancy Mannigoe's worthless nigger life——

She stops speaking, sitting quite still, erect in the chair, her face raised slightly, not looking at either of them while they watch her.

GOVERNOR
Give her the handkerchief now.

Stevens takes a fresh handkerchief from his pocket, shakes it out and extends it toward Temple. She does not move, her hands still clasped in her lap. Stevens rises, crosses, drops the handkerchief into her lap, returns to his chair.

TEMPLE
Thanks really. But it doesn't matter now; we're too near the end; you could almost go on down to the car and start it and have the engine warming up while I finish.

(to Governor)

You see? All you'll have to do now is just be still and listen. Or not even listen if you don't want to: but just be still, just wait. And not long either now. and then we can all go to bed and turn off the light. And then, night: dark, sleep even maybe, when with the same arm you turn off the light and pull the covers up with, you can put away forever Temple Drake and whatever it is you have done about her, and Nancy Mannigoe and whatever it is you have done about her, if you're going to do anything, if it even matters anyhow whether you do anything or not, and none of it will ever have to bother us any more. Because Uncle Gavin was only partly right. It's not that you must never even look on evil and corruption; sometimes you can't help that, you are not always warned. It's not even that you must resist it always. Because you've got to start much sooner than that. You've got to be already prepared to resist it, say no to it, long before you see it; you must have already said no to it long before you even know what it is. I'll have the cigarette now, please.

Stevens takes up the pack, rising and working the end of a cigarette free, and extends the pack. She takes the cigarette, already speaking again while Stevens puts the pack on the desk and takes up the lighter which the Governor, watching Temple, shoves across the desk where Stevens can reach it. Stevens snaps the lighter on and holds it out. Temple makes no effort to light the cigarette, holding the cigarette in her hand and talking. Then she lays the cigarette unlighted on the ashtray and Stevens closes the lighter and sits down again, putting the lighter down beside the pack of cigarettes.

Because Temple Drake liked evil. She only went to the ball game because she would have to get on a train to do it, so that she could slip off the train the first time it stopped, and get into the car to drive a hundred miles with a man——

STEVENS

—who couldn't hold his drink.

TEMPLE
(to Stevens)
All right. Aren't I just saying that?
(to Governor)
An optimist. Not the young man; he was just doing the best he knew, could. It wasn't him that suggested the trip: it was Temple——

STEVENS

It was his car though. Or his mother's.

TEMPLE
(to Stevens)
All right. All right.
(to Governor)
No, Temple was the optimist: not that she had foreseen, planned ahead either: she just had unbounded faith that her father and brothers would know evil when they saw it, so all she had to do was, do the one thing which she knew they would forbid her to do if they had the chance. And they were right about the evil, and so of course she was right too, though even then it was not easy: she

even had to drive the car for a while after we
began to realise that the young man was wrong,
had graduated too soon in the drinking part of his
Virginia training——

STEVENS

It was Gowan who knew the moonshiner and
insisted on going there.

TEMPLE

—and even then——

STEVENS

He was driving when you wrecked.

TEMPLE

(to Stevens: quick and harsh)
And married me for it. Does he have to pay for it
twice? It wasn't really worth paying for once,
was it?

(to Governor)
And even then——

GOVERNOR

How much was it worth?

TEMPLE

Was what worth?

GOVERNOR

His marrying you.

TEMPLE

You mean to him, of course. Less than he paid
for it.

GOVERNOR

Is that what he thinks too?

> (they stare at one another, Temple alert,
> quite watchful, though rather impatient
> than anything else)

You're going to tell me something that he doesn't know, else you would have brought him with you. Is that right?

TEMPLE

Yes.

GOVERNOR

Would you tell it if he were here?

> (Temple is staring at the Governor. Un-
> noticed by her, Stevens makes a faint
> movement. The Governor stops him
> with a slight motion of one hand which
> also Temple does not notice)

Now that you have come this far, now that, as you said, you have got to tell it, say it aloud, not to save Nan—this woman, but because you decided before you left home tonight that there is nothing else to do but tell it.

TEMPLE

How do I know whether I would or not?

GOVERNOR

Suppose he was here—sitting in that chair where Gav—your uncle is——

TEMPLE

—or behind the door or in one of your desk

drawers, maybe? He's not. He's at home. I gave
him a sleeping pill.

GOVERNOR

But suppose he was, now that you have got to say
it. Would you still say it?

TEMPLE

All right. Yes. Now will you please shut up too
and let me tell it? How can I, if you and Gavin
won't hush and let me? I can't even remember
where I was.—Oh yes. So I saw the murder, or
anyway the shadow of it, and the man took me to
Memphis, and I know that too, I had two legs and
I could see, and I could have simply screamed up
the main street of any of the little towns we
passed, just as I could have walked away from the
car after Gow—we ran it into the tree, and stopped
a wagon or a car which would have carried me to
the nearest town or railroad station or even back
to school or, for that matter, right on back home
into my father's or brothers' hands. But not me,
not Temple. I chose the murderer——

STEVENS

(to Governor)

He was a psychopath, though that didn't come out
in the trial, and when it did come out, or could
have come out, it was too late. I was there; I saw
that too: a little black thing with an Italian name,
like a neat and only slightly deformed cockroach:
a hybrid, sexually incapable. But then, she will tell
you that too.

TEMPLE
(with bitter sarcasm)
Dear Uncle Gavin.
(to Governor)
Oh yes, that too, her bad luck too: to plump for
a thing which didn't even have sex for his weak-
ness, but just murder——
(she stops, sitting motionless, erect, her
hands clenched on her lap, her eyes
closed)
If you both would just hush, just let me, I seem to
be like trying to drive a hen into a barrel. Maybe
if you would just try to act like you wanted to
keep her out of it, from going into it——

GOVERNOR
Don't call it a barrel. Call it a tunnel. That's a
thoroughfare, because the other end is open too.
Go through it. There was no—sex.

TEMPLE
Not from him. He was worse than a father or
uncle. It was worse than being the wealthy ward
of the most indulgent trust or insurance company:
carried to Memphis and shut up in that Manuel
Street sporting house like a ten-year-old bride in a
Spanish convent, with the madam herself more
eagle-eyed than any mama—and the Negro maid
to guard the door while the madam would be out,
to wherever she would go, wherever the madams
of cat houses go on their afternoons out, to pay
police-court fines or protection or to the bank or
maybe just visiting, which would not be so bad

because the maid would unlock the door and
come inside and we could——

> (she falters, pauses for less than a second;
> then quickly)

Yes, that's why—talk. A prisoner of course, and
maybe not in a very gilded cage, but at least the
prisoner was. I had perfume by the quart; some
salesgirl chose it of course, and it was the wrong
kind, but at least I had it, and he bought me a fur
coat—with nowhere to wear it of course because
he wouldn't let me out, but I had the coat—and
snazzy underwear and negligees, selected also by
salesgirls but at least the best or anyway the most
expensive—the taste at least of the big end of an
underworld big shot's wallet. Because he wanted
me to be contented, you see; and not only contented, he didn't even mind if I was happy too:
just so I was there when or in case the police finally
connected him with that Mississippi murder; not
only didn't mind if I was happy; he even made the
effort himself to see that I was. And so at last we
have come to it, because now I have got to tell you
this too to give you a valid reason why I waked
you up at two in the morning to ask you to save
a murderess.

She stops speaking, reaches and takes the unlighted cigarette from the tray, then realises it is unlit. Stevens takes
up the lighter from the desk and starts to get up. Still
watching Temple, the Governor makes to Stevens a
slight arresting signal with his hand. Stevens pauses, then
pushes the lighter along the desk to where Temple can
reach it, and sits back down. Temple takes the lighter,

snaps it on, lights the cigarette, closes the lighter and puts
it back on the desk. But after only one puff at the
cigarette, she lays it back on the tray and sits again as
before, speaking again.

Because I still had the two arms and legs and eyes;
I could have climbed down the rainspout at any
time, the only difference being that I didn't. I
would never leave the room except late at night,
when he would come in a closed car the size of an
undertaker's wagon, and he and the chauffeur on
the front seat, and me and the madam in the back,
rushing at forty and fifty and sixty miles an hour
up and down the back alleys of the redlight district. Which—the back alleys—was all I ever saw
of them too. I was not even permitted to meet or
visit with or even see the other girls in my own
house, not even to sit with them after work and
listen to the shop talk while they counted their
chips or blisters or whatever they would do sitting
on one another's beds in the elected dormitory. . . .

(she pauses again, continues in a sort of
surprise, amazement)

Yes, it was like the dormitory at school: the smell:
of women, young women all busy thinking not
about men but just man: only a little stronger, a
little calmer, less excited—sitting on the tem-
porarily idle beds discussing the exigencies—that's
surely the right one, isn't it?—of their trade. But
not me, not Temple: shut up in that room twenty-
four hours a day, with nothing to do but hold
fashion shows in the fur coat and the flashy pants
and negligees, with nothing to see it but a two-

foot mirror and a Negro maid; hanging bone dry and safe in the middle of sin and pleasure like being suspended twenty fathoms deep in an ocean diving bell. Because he wanted her to be contented, you see. He even made the last effort himself. But Temple didn't want to be just contented. So she had to do what us sporting girls call fall in love.

GOVERNOR

Ah.

STEVENS

That's right.

TEMPLE
(quickly: to Stevens)
Hush.

STEVENS
(to Temple)
Hush yourself.
(to Governor)
He—Vitelli—they called him Popeye—brought the man there himself. He—the young man——

TEMPLE

Gavin! No, I tell you!

STEVENS
(to Temple)
You are drowning in an orgasm of abjectness and moderation when all you need is truth.
(to Governor)
—was known in his own circles as Red, Alabama Red; not to the police, or not officially, since he

E

was not a criminal, or anyway not yet, but just a thug, probably cursed more by simple eupepsia than by anything else. He was a houseman—the bouncer—at the nightclub, joint, on the outskirts of town, which Popeye owned and which was Popeye's headquarters. He died shortly afterward in the alley behind Temple's prison, of a bullet from the same pistol which had done the Mississippi murder, though Popeye too was dead, hanged in Alabama for a murder he did not commit, before the pistol was ever found and connected with him.

GOVERNOR
I see. This—Popeye——

STEVENS
—discovered himself betrayed by one of his own servants, and took a princely vengeance on his honour's smircher? You will be wrong. You underrate this *précieux*, this flower, this jewel. Vitelli. What a name for him. A hybrid, impotent. He was hanged the next year, to be sure. But even that was wrong: his very effacement debasing, flouting, even what dignity man has been able to lend to necessary human abolishment. He should have been crushed somehow under a vast and mindless boot, like a spider. He didn't sell her; you violate and outrage his very memory with that crass and material impugnment. He was a purist, an amateur always: he did not even murder for base profit. It was not even for simple lust. He was a gourmet, a sybarite, centuries, perhaps hemi-

spheres before his time; in spirit and glands he was of that age of princely despots to whom the ability even to read was vulgar and plebeian and, reclining on silk amid silken airs and scents, had eunuch slaves for that office, commanding death to the slave at the end of each reading, each evening, that none else alive, even a eunuch slave, shall have shared in, partaken of, remembered, the poem's evocation.

GOVERNOR
I don't think I understand.

STEVENS
Try to. Uncheck your capacity for rage and revulsion—the sort of rage and revulsion it takes to step on a worm. If Vitelli cannot evoke that in you, his life will have been indeed a desert.

TEMPLE
Or don't try to. Just let it go. Just for God's sake let it go. I met the man, how doesn't matter, and I fell what I called in love with him and what it was or what I called it doesn't matter either because all that matters is that I wrote the letters——

GOVERNOR
I see. This is the part that her husband didn't know.

TEMPLE
(to Governor)
And what does that matter either? Whether he knows or not? What can another face or two or

name or two matter, since he knows that I lived
for six weeks in a Manuel Street brothel? Or
another body or two in the bed? Or three or four?
I'm trying to tell it, enough of it. Can't you see
that?   But can't you make him let me alone so I
can. Make him, for God's sake, let me alone.

GOVERNOR
(to Stevens: watching Temple)
No more, Gavin.
(to Temple)
So you fell in love.

TEMPLE
Thank you for that. I mean, the 'love.' Except that
I didn't even fall, I was already there: the bad, the
lost: who could have climbed down the gutter or
lightning rod any time and got away, or even
simpler than that: disguised myself as the nigger
maid with a stack of towels and a bottle opener
and change for ten dollars, and walked right out
the front door. So I wrote the letters. I would
write one each time . . . afterward, after they—he
left, and sometimes I would write two or three
when it would be two or three days between,
when they—he wouldn't——

GOVERNOR
What? What's that?

TEMPLE
—you know: something to do, be doing, filling
the time, better than the fashion parades in front
of the two-foot glass with nobody to be disturbed

even by the . . . pants, or even no pants. Good letters——

GOVERNOR

Wait. What did you say?

TEMPLE

I said they were good letters, even for——

GOVERNOR

You said, after *they* left.
> (they look at one another. Temple
> doesn't answer: to Stevens, though still
> watching Temple)

Am I being told that this . . . Vitelli would be there in the room too?

STEVENS

Yes. That was why he brought him. You can see now what I meant by connoisseur and gourmet.

GOVERNOR

And what you meant by the boot too. But he's dead. You know that.

STEVENS

Oh yes. He's dead. And I said 'purist' too. To the last: hanged the next summer in Alabama for a murder he didn't even commit and which nobody involved in the matter really believed he had committed, only not even his lawyer could persuade him to admit that he couldn't have done it if he had wanted to, or wouldn't have done it if the notion had struck him. Oh yes, he's dead too; we haven't come here for vengeance.

GOVERNOR
(to Temple)
Yes. Go on. The letters.

TEMPLE

The letters. They were good letters. I mean—good
ones.
(staring steadily at the Governor)
What I'm trying to say is, they were the kind of
letters that if you had written them to a man, even
eight years ago, you wouldn't—would—rather
your husband didn't see them, no matter what he
thought about your—past.
(still staring at the Governor as she makes
her painful confession)
Better than you would expect from a seventeen-
year-old amateur. I mean, you would have won-
dered how anybody just seventeen and not even
through freshman in college, could have learned
the—right words. Though all you would have
needed probably would be an old dictionary from
back in Shakespeare's time when, so they say,
people hadn't learned how to blush at words.
That is, anybody except Temple Drake, who
didn't need a dictionary, who was a fast learner
and so even just one lesson would have been
enough for her, let alone three or four or a dozen
or two or three dozen.
(staring at the Governor)
No, not even one lesson because the bad was
already there waiting, who hadn't even heard yet
that you must be already resisting the corruption

not only before you look at it but before you even know what it is, what you are resisting. So I wrote the letters, I don't know how many, enough, more than enough because just one would have been enough. And that's all.

GOVERNOR

All?

TEMPLE

Yes. You've certainly heard of blackmail. The letters turned up again of course. And of course, being Temple Drake, the first way to buy them back that Temple Drake thought of, was to produce the material for another set of them.

STEVENS

(to Temple)

Yes, that's all. But you've got to tell him why it's all.

TEMPLE

I thought I had. I wrote some letters that you would have thought that even Temple Drake might have been ashamed to put on paper, and then the man I wrote them to died, and I married another man and reformed, or thought I had, and bore two children and hired another reformed whore so that I would have somebody to talk to, and I even thought I had forgotten about the letters until they turned up again and then I found out that I not only hadn't forgot about the letters, I hadn't even reformed——

STEVENS

All right. Do you want me to tell it, then?

TEMPLE

And you were the one preaching moderation.

STEVENS

I was preaching against orgasms of it.

TEMPLE
(bitterly)

Oh, I know. Just suffering. Not for anything: just suffering. Just because it's good for you, like calomel or ipecac.
(to Governor)

All right. What?

GOVERNOR

The young man died——

TEMPLE

Oh yes.—Died, shot from a car while he was slipping up the alley behind the house, to climb up the same drainpipe I could have climbed down at any time and got away, to see me—the one time, the first time, the only time when we thought we had dodged, fooled him, could be alone together, just the two of us, after all the . . . other ones.—If love can be, mean anything, except the newness, the learning, the peace, the privacy: no shame: not even conscious that you are naked because you are just using the nakedness because that's a part of it; then he was dead, killed, shot down right in the middle of thinking about me, when in just one more minute maybe he would have been in the room with me, when all of him except just his body was already in the

room with me and the door locked at last for just
the two of us alone; and then it was all over and
as though it had never been, happened: it had to
be as though it had never happened, except that
that was even worse——
            (rapidly)
Then the courtroom in Jefferson and I didn't care,
not about anything any more, and my father and
brothers waiting and then the year in Europe,
Paris, and I still didn't care, and then after a while
it really did get easier. You know. People are
lucky. They are wonderful. At first you think that
you can bear only so much and then you will be
free. Then you find out that you can bear anything, you really can and then it won't even
matter. Because suddenly it could be as if it had
never been, never happened. You know: somebody—Hemingway, wasn't it?—wrote a book
about how it had never actually happened to a
gir—woman, if she just refused to accept it, no
matter who remembered, bragged. And besides,
the ones who could—remember—were both dead.
Then Gowan came to Paris that winter and we
were married—at the Embassy, with a reception
afterward at the Crillon, and if that couldn't
fumigate an American past, what else this side of
heaven could you hope for to remove stink? Not to
mention a new automobile and a honeymoon in a
rented hideaway built for his European mistress by
a Mohammedan prince at Cap Ferrat. Only——
            (she pauses, falters, for just an instant,
            then goes on)

                                                    E*

—we—I thought we—I didn't want to efface the
stink really——

> (rapidly now, tense, erect, her hands
> gripped again into fists on her lap)

You know: just the marriage would be enough:
not the Embassy and the Crillon and Cap Ferrat but
just to kneel down, the two of us, and say 'We have
sinned, forgive us.' And then maybe there would
be the love this time—the peace, the quiet, the no
shame that I . . . didn't—missed that other time——

> (falters again, then rapidly again, glib
> and succinct)

Love, but more than love too: not depending on
just love to hold two people together, make them
better than either one would have been alone, but
tragedy, suffering, having suffered and caused
grief; having something to have to live with even
when, because you knew both of you could never
forget it. And then I began to believe something
even more than that: that there was something
even better, stronger, than tragedy to hold two
people together: forgiveness. Only that seemed to
be wrong. Only maybe it wasn't the forgiveness
that was wrong, but the gratitude; and maybe the
only thing worse than having to give gratitude
constantly all the time, is having to accept it——

STEVENS

Which is exactly backward. What was wrong
wasn't——

GOVERNOR

Gavin.

STEVENS

Shut up yourself, Henry. What was wrong wasn't
Temple's good name. It wasn't even her husband's
conscience. It was his vanity: the Virginia-trained
aristocrat caught with his gentility around his
knees like the guest in the trick Hollywood bathroom. So the forgiving wasn't enough for him,
or perhaps he hadn't read Hemingway's book.
Because after about a year, his restiveness under
the onus of accepting the gratitude began to take
the form of doubting the paternity of their child

TEMPLE

Oh God. Oh God.

GOVERNOR

Gavin.
          (Stevens stops.)
No more, I said. Call that an order.
          (to Temple)
Yes. Tell me.

TEMPLE

I'm trying to. I expected our main obstacle in
this would be the bereaved plaintiff. Apparently
though it's the defendant's lawyer. I mean, I'm
trying to tell you about one Temple Drake, and
our Uncle Gavin is showing you another one. So
already you've got two different people begging
for the same clemency; if everybody concerned
keeps on splitting up into two people, you won't
even know who to pardon, will you? And now
that I mention it, here we are, already back to

Nancy Mannigoe, and now surely it shouldn't take long. Let's see, we'd got back to Jefferson too, hadn't we? Anyway, we are now. I mean, back in Jefferson, back home. You know: face it: the disgrace: the shame, face it down, good and down forever, never to haunt us more; together, a common front to stink because we love each other and have forgiven all, strong in our love and mutual forgiveness. Besides having everything else: the Gowan Stevenses, young, popular: a new bungalow on the right street to start the Saturday night hangovers in, a country club with a country-club younger set of rallying friends to make it a Saturday-night hangover worthy the name of Saturday-night country-club hangover, a pew in the right church to recover from it in, provided of course they were not too hungover even to get to church. Then the son and heir came; and now we have Nancy: nurse: guide: mentor, catalyst, glue, whatever you want to call it, holding the whole lot of them together—not just a magnetic centre for the heir apparent and the other little princes or princesses in their orderly succession, to circle around, but for the two bigger hunks too of mass or matter or dirt or whatever it is shaped in the image of God, in a semblance at least of order and respectability and peace; not ole cradle-rocking black mammy at all, because the Gowan Stevenses are young and modern, so young and modern that all the other young country-club set applauded when they took an ex-dope-fiend nigger whore out of the gutter to nurse their children, because

the rest of the young country-club set didn't know
that it wasn't the Gowan Stevenses but Temple
Drake who had chosen the ex-dope-fiend nigger
whore for the reason that an ex-dope-fiend nigger
whore was the only animal in Jefferson that spoke
Temple Drake's language——

> (quickly takes up the burning cigarette
> from the tray and puffs at it, talking
> through the puffs)

Oh yes, I'm going to tell this too. A confidante.
You know: the big-time ball player, the idol on
the pedestal, the worshipped; and the worshipper,
the acolyte, the one that never had and never
would, no matter how willing or how hard she
tried, get out of the sandlots, the bush league. You
know: the long afternoons, with the last electric
button pressed on the last cooking or washing or
sweeping gadget and the baby safely asleep for a
while, and the two sisters in sin swapping trade
or anyway avocational secrets over Coca-Colas in
the quiet kitchen. Somebody to talk to, as we all
seem to need, want, have to have, not to converse
with you nor even agree with you, but just keep
quiet and listen. Which is all that people really
want, really need; I mean, to behave themselves,
keep out of one another's hair; the maladjustments
which they tell us breed the arsonists and rapists
and murderers and thieves and the rest of the anti-
social enemies, are not really maladjustments but
simply because the embryonic murderers and
thieves didn't have anybody to listen to them:
which is an idea the Catholic Church discovered

two thousand years ago only it just didn't carry it
far enough or maybe it was too busy being the
Church to have time to bother with man, or
maybe it wasn't the Church's fault at all but
simply because it had to deal with human beings
and maybe if the world was just populated with
a kind of creature half of which were dumb,
couldn't do anything but listen, couldn't even
escape from having to listen to the other half,
there wouldn't even be any war. Which was what
Temple had: somebody paid by the week, just to
listen, which you would have thought would have
been enough; and then the other baby came, the
infant, the doomed sacrifice (though of course we
don't know that yet) and you would have thought
that this was surely enough, that now even Temple
Drake would consider herself safe, could be
depended on, having two—what do sailors call
them? oh yes, sheet-anchors—now. Only it wasn't
enough. Because Hemingway was right. I mean,
the gir—woman in his book. All you have got
to do is, refuse to accept. Only, you have got to
. . . refuse——

STEVENS

Now, the letters——

GOVERNOR
(watching Temple)
Be quiet, Gavin.

STEVENS

No, I'm going to talk a while now. We'll even

stick to the sports metaphor and call it a relay race,
with the senior member of the team carrying the
. . . baton, twig, switch, sapling, tree—whatever
you want to call the symbolical wood, up what
remains of the symbolical hill.

> (the lights flicker, grow slightly dimmer,
> then flare back up and steady again, as
> though in a signal, a warning)

The letters. The blackmail. The blackmailer was
Red's younger brother—a criminal of course, but
at least a man——

TEMPLE

No! No!

STEVENS
(to Temple)

Be quiet too. It only goes up a hill, not over a
precipice. Besides, it's only a stick. The letters were
not first. The first thing was the gratitude. And
now we have even come to the husband, my
nephew. And when I say 'past,' I mean that part
of it which the husband knows so far, which
apparently was enough in his estimation. Because
it was not long before she discovered, realised, that
she was going to spend a good part of the rest
of her days (nights too) being forgiven for it; in
being not only constantly reminded—well, maybe
not specifically reminded, but say made—kept—
aware of it in order to be forgiven for it so that
she might be grateful to the forgiver, but in having
to employ more and more of what tact she had—
and the patience which she probably didn't know

she had, since until now she had never occasion to
need patience—to make the gratitude—in which
she had probably had as little experience as she
had had with patience—acceptable to meet with,
match, the high standards of the forgiver. But she
was not too concerned. Her husband—my nephew
—had made what he probably considered the
supreme sacrifice to expiate his part in her past;
she had no doubts of her capacity to continue to
supply whatever increasing degree of gratitude the
increasing appetite—or capacity—of its addict
would demand, in return for the sacrifice which,
so she believed, she had accepted for the same
reason of gratitude. Besides, she still had the legs
and the eyes; she could walk away, escape, from
it at any moment she wished, even though her
past might have shown her that she probably would not use the ability to locomote to
escape from threat and danger. Do you accept
that?

GOVERNOR
All right. Go on.

STEVENS
Then she discovered that the child—the first one
—was on the way. For that first instant, she must
have known something almost like frenzy. Now
she couldn't escape; she had waited too long. But
it was worse than that. It was as though she
realised for the first time that you—everyone—
must, or anyway may have to, pay for your past;
that past is something like a promissory note with

a trick clause in it which, as long as nothing goes wrong, can be manumitted in an orderly manner, but which fate or luck or chance can foreclose on you without warning. That is, she had known, accepted, this all the time and dismissed it because she knew that she could cope, was invulnerable through simple integration, own-womanness. But now there would be a child, tender and defence-less. But you never really give up hope, you know, not even after you finally realise that people not only can bear anything, but probably will have to, so probably even before the frenzy had had time to fade, she found a hope: which was the child's own tender and defenceless innocence: that God —if there was one—would protect the child—not her: she asked no quarter and wanted none; she could cope, either cope or bear it, but the child from the sight draft of her past—because it was innocent, even though she knew better, all her observation having shown her that God either would not or could not—anyway, did not—save innocence just because it was innocent; that when He said 'Suffer little children to come unto Me' He meant exactly that: He meant suffer; that the adults, the fathers, the old in and capable of sin, must be ready and willing—nay, eager—to suffer at any time, that the little children shall come unto Him unanguished, unterrified, undefiled. Do you accept that?

GOVERNOR

Go on.

STEVENS

So at least she had ease. Not hope: ease. It was
precarious of course, a balance, but she could walk
a tight-rope too. It was as though she had struck,
not a bargain, but an armistice with God—if there
was one. She had not tried to cheat; she had not
tried to evade the promissory note of her past by
intervening the blank cheque of a child's innocence
—it was born now, a little boy, a son, her husband's son and heir—between. She had not tried to
prevent the child; she had simply never thought
about pregnancy in this connection, since it took
the physical fact of the pregnancy to reveal to her
the existence of that promissory note bearing her
post-dated signature. And since God—if there was
one—must be aware of that, then she too would
bear her side of the bargain by not demanding on
Him a second time since He—if there was one—
would at least play fair, would be at least a gentleman. And that?

GOVERNOR

Go on.

STEVENS

So you can take your choice about the second
child. Perhaps she was too busy between the three
of them to be careful enough: between the three
of them: the doom, the fate, the past; the bargain
with God; the forgiveness and the gratitude. Like
the juggler says, not with three insentient replace-
able Indian clubs or balls, but three glass bulbs
filled with nitroglycerine and not enough hands

for one even: one hand to offer the atonement
with and another to receive the forgiveness with
and a third needed to offer the gratitude, and still
a fourth hand more and more imperative as time
passed to sprinkle in steadily and constantly increasing doses a little more and a little more of the
sugar and seasoning on the gratitude to keep it
palatable to its swallower—that perhaps: she just
didn't have time to be careful enough, or perhaps
it was desperation, or perhaps this was when
her husband first refuted or implied or anyway
impugned—whichever it was—his son's paternity.
Anyway, she was pregnant again; she had broken
her word, destroyed her talisman, and she probably knew fifteen months before the letters that
this was the end, and when the man appeared with
the old letters she probably was not even surprised:
she had merely been wondering for fifteen months
what form the doom would take. And accept this
too——

The lights flicker and dim further, then steady at that
point.

And relief too. Because at last it was over; the roof
had fallen, avalanche had roared; even the help-
lessness and the impotence were finished now, because now even the old fragility of bone and meat
was no longer a factor—and, who knows? because
of that fragility, a kind of pride, triumph: you have
waited for destruction: you endured; it was inevitable, inescapable, you had no hope. Nevertheless,
you did not merely cringe, crouching, your head,
vision, buried in your arms; you were not watch-

ing that poised arrestment all the time, true enough, but that was not because you feared it but because you were too busy putting one foot before the other, never for one instant really flagging, faltering, even though you knew it was in vain—triumph in the very fragility which no longer need concern you now, for the reason that the all, the very worst, which catastrophe can do to you, is crush and obliterate the fragility; you were the better man, you outfaced even catastrophe, outlasted it, compelled it to move first; you did not even defy it, not even contemptuous: with no other tool or implement but that worthless fragility, you held disaster off as with one hand you might support the weightless silken canopy of a bed, for six long years while it, with all its weight and power, could not possibly prolong the obliteration of your fragility over five or six seconds; and even during that five or six seconds you would still be the better man, since all that it—the catastrophe—could deprive you of, you yourself had already written off six years ago as being, inherently of and because of its own fragile self, worthless.

GOVERNOR

And now, the man.

STEVENS

I thought you would see it too. Even the first one stuck out like a sore thumb. Yes, he——

GOVERNOR

The first what?

STEVENS
(pauses, looks at the Governor)

The first man: Red. Don't you know anything at
all about women? I never saw Red or this next
one, his brother, either, but all three of them, the
other two and her husband, probably all look
enough alike or act enough alike—maybe by
simply making enough impossible unfulfillable
demands on her or by being drawn to her enough
to accept, risk, almost incredible conditions—to
be at least first cousins. Where have you been all
your life?

GOVERNOR

All right. The man.

STEVENS

At first, all he thought of, planned on, was interested in, intended, was the money—to collect
for the letters, and beat it, get the hell out. Of
course, even at the end, all he was really after was
still the money, not only after he found out that
he would have to take her and the child too to get
it, but even when it looked like all he was going
to get, at least for a while, was just a runaway wife
and a six-months-old infant. In fact, Nancy's error,
her really fatal action on that fatal and tragic night,
was in not giving the money and the jewels both
to him when she found where Temple had hidden
them, and getting the letters and getting rid of him
forever, instead of hiding the money and jewels
from Temple in her turn—which was what
Temple herself thought too apparently, since she

—Temple—told him a lie about how much the
money was, telling him it was only two hundred
dollars when it was actually almost two thousand.
So you would have said that he wanted the money
indeed, and just how much, how badly, to have
been willing to pay that price for it. Or maybe he
was being wise—'smart,' he would have called it
—beyond his years and time, and without having
actually planned it that way, was really inventing
a new and safe method of kidnapping: that is, pick
an adult victim capable of signing her own cheques
—also with an infant in arms for added persuasion
—and not forcing but actually persuading her to
come along under her own power and then—still
peaceably—extracting the money later at your
leisure, using the tender welfare of the infant as a
fulcrum for your lever. Or maybe we're both
wrong and both should give credit—what little of
it—where credit—what little of it—is due, since it
was just the money with her too at first, though
he was probably still thinking it was just the
money at the very time when, having got her own
jewellery together and found where her husband
kept the key to the strongbox (and I imagine, even
opened it one night after her husband was in bed
asleep and counted the money in it or at least
made sure there was money in it or anyway that
the key would actually open it), she found herself
still trying to rationalise why she had not paid over
the money and got the letters and destroyed them
and so rid herself forever of her Damocles' roof.
Which was what she did not do. Because Heming-

way—his girl—was quite right: all you have got to
do is, refuse to accept it. Only, you have got to be
told truthfully beforehand what you must refuse;
the gods owe you that—at least a clear picture
and a clear choice. Not to be fooled by . . . who
knows? probably even gentleness, after a fashion,
back there on those afternoons or whenever they
were in the Memphis . . . all right: honeymoon,
even with a witness; in this case certainly anything
much better lacked, and indeed, who knows? (I
am Red now) even a little of awe, incredulous
hope, incredulous amazement, even a little of
trembling at this much fortune, this much luck
dropping out of the very sky itself, into his
embrace; at least (Temple now) no gang; even
rape become tender: only one, an individual, still
refusable, giving her at least (this time) the simili-
tude of being wooed, of an opportunity to say Yes
first, letting her even believe she could say either
one of yes or no. I imagine that he (the new one,
the blackmailer) even looked like his brother—a
younger Red, the Red of a few years even before
she knew him, and—if you will permit it—less
stained, so that in a way it may have seemed to her
that here at last even she might slough away the
six years' soilure of struggle and repentance and
terror to no avail. And if this is what you meant,
then you are right too: a man, at least a man, after
six years of that sort of forgiving which debased
not only the forgiven but the forgiven's gratitude
too—a bad man of course, a criminal by intent
regardless of how cramped his opportunities may

have been up to this moment; and, capable of blackmail, vicious and not merely competent to, but destined to, bring nothing but evil and disaster and ruin to anyone foolish enough to enter his orbit, cast her lot with his. But—by comparison, that six years of comparison—at least a man—a man so single, so hard and ruthless, so impeccable in amorality, as to have a kind of integrity, purity, who would not only never need nor intend to forgive anyone anything, he would never even realise that anyone expected him to forgive anyone anything; who wouldn't even bother to forgive her if it ever dawned on him that he had the opportunity, but instead would simply black her eyes and knock a few teeth out and fling her into the gutter: so that she could rest secure forever in the knowledge that, until she found herself with a black eye and or spitting teeth in the gutter, he would never even know he had anything to forgive her for.

This time, the lights do not flicker. They begin to dim steadily toward and then into complete darkness as Stevens continues.

Nancy was the confidante, at first, while she— Nancy—still believed probably that the only problem, factor, was how to raise the money the blackmailer demanded, without letting the boss, the master, the husband find out about it; finding, discovering—this is still Nancy—realising probably that she had not really been a confidante for a good while, a long while before she discovered that what she actually was, was a spy: on her

employer: not realising until after she had discovered that, although Temple had taken the
money and the jewels too from her husband's
strongbox, she—Temple—still hadn't paid them
over to the blackmailer and got the letters, that
the payment of the money and jewels was less than
half of Temple's plan.

The lights go completely out. The stage is in complete
darkness. Stevens' voice continues.

That was when Nancy in her turn found where
Temple had hidden the money and jewels, and
—Nancy—took them in her turn and hid them
from Temple; this was the night of the day
Gowan left for a week's fishing at Aransas Pass,
taking the older child, the boy, with him, to leave
the child for a week's visit with its grandparents
in New Orleans until Gowan would pick him up
on his way home from Texas.

(to Temple: in the darkness)
Now tell him.

The stage is in complete darkness.

Interior, Temple's private sitting- or dressing-room.
9.30 P.M. September thirteenth *ante*.

The lights go up, lower right, as in Act I in the transition
from the Courtroom to the Stevenses' living-room,
though instead of the living-room, the scene is now
Temple's private apartment. A door, left, enters from the
house proper. A door, right, leads into the nursery where
the child is asleep in its crib. At rear, french-windows
open on to a terrace; this is a private entrance to the
house itself from outside. At left, a cupboard door stands
open. Garments are scattered over the floor about it,
indicating that the cupboard has been searched, not
hurriedly so much as savagely and ruthlessly and thoroughly. At right, is a fireplace of gas logs. A desk against
the rear wall is open and shows traces of the same savage
and ruthless search. A table, centre, bears Temple's hat,
gloves and bag, also a bag such as is associated with
infants; two cases, obviously Temple's, are packed and
closed and sit on the floor beside the table. The whole
room indicates Temple's imminent departure, and that
something has been vainly yet savagely and completely,
perhaps even frantically, searched for.

When the lights go up, Pete is standing in the open
cupboard door, holding a final garment, a negligee, in his
hands. He is about twenty-five. He does not look like a
criminal. That is, he is not a standardised recognisable
criminal or gangster type, quite. He looks almost like the
general conception of a college man, or a successful
young automobile or appliance salesman. His clothes are

ordinary, neither flashy nor sharp, simply what everybody wears. But there is a definite 'untamed' air to him. He is handsome, attractive to women, not at all unpredictable because you—or they—know exactly what he will do, you just hope he won't do it this time. He has a hard, ruthless quality, not immoral but unmoral.

He wears a light-weight summer suit, his hat is shoved on to the back of his head so that, engaged as he is at present, he looks exactly like a youthful city detective in a tough moving picture. He is searching the flimsy negligee, quickly and without gentleness, drops it and turns, finds his feet entangled in the other garments on the floor and without pausing, kicks himself free and crosses to the desk and stands looking down at the litter on it which he has already searched thoroughly and savagely once, with a sort of bleak and contemptuous disgust.

Temple enters, left. She wears a dark suit for travelling beneath a lightweight open coat, is hatless, carries the fur coat which we have seen, and a child's robe or blanket over the same arm, and a filled milk bottle in the other hand. She pauses long enough to glance at the littered room. Then she comes on in and approaches the table. Pete turns his head; except for that, he doesn't move.

PETE

Well?

TEMPLE

No. The people where she lives say they haven't seen her since she left to come to work this morning.

                         PETE

I could have told you that.
          (he glances at his wrist watch)
We've still got time. Where does she live?

                        TEMPLE
          (at the table)
And then what? hold a lighted cigarette against
the sole of her foot?

                         PETE

It's fifty dollars, even if you are accustomed yourself to thinking in hundreds. Besides the jewellery.
What do you suggest then? call the cops?

                        TEMPLE

No. You won't have to run. I'm giving you an
out.

                         PETE

An out?

                        TEMPLE

No, dough, no snatch. Isn't that how you would
say it?

                         PETE

Maybe I don't get you.

                        TEMPLE

You can quit now. Clear out. Leave. Get out from
under. Save yourself. Then all you'll have to do is,
wait till my husband gets back, and start over.

                         PETE

Maybe I still don't get you.

TEMPLE

You've still got the letters, haven't you?

PETE

Oh, the letters.

He reaches inside his coat, takes out the packet of letters and tosses it onto the table.

There you are.

TEMPLE

I told you two days ago I didn't want them.

PETE

Sure. That was two days ago.

They watch each other a moment. Then Temple dumps the fur coat and the robe from her arm, onto the table, sets the bottle carefully on the table, takes up the packet of letters and extends her other hand to Pete.

TEMPLE

Give me your lighter.

Pete produces the lighter from his pocket and hands it to her. That is, he extends it, not moving otherwise, so that she has to take a step or two toward him to reach and take it. Then she turns and crosses to the hearth, snaps the lighter on. It misses fire two or three times, then lights. Pete has not moved, watching her. She stands motionless a moment, the packet of letters in one hand, the burning lighter in the other. Then she turns her head and looks back at him. For another moment they watch each other.

PETE

Go ahead. Burn them. The other time I gave them to you, you turned them down so you could

always change your mind and back out. Burn
them.

They watch each other for another moment. Then she
turns her head and stands now, her face averted, the lighter
still burning. Pete watches her for another moment.

Then put that junk down and come here.

She snaps out the lighter, turns, crosses to the table, putting the packet of letters and the lighter on the table as
she passes it, and goes on to where Pete has not moved.
At this moment, Nancy appears in the door, left. Neither
of them sees her. Pete puts his arms around Temple.

I offered you an out too.
                    (he draws her closer)
Baby.

TEMPLE
Don't call me that.

PETE
                    (tightens his arms, caressing and savage
                    too)

Red did. I'm as good a man as he was. Ain't I?
They kiss. Nancy moves quietly through the door and
stops just inside the room, watching them. She now wears
the standardised department-store maidservant's uniform,
but without cap and apron, beneath a light-weight open
topcoat; on her head is a battered almost shapeless felt hat
which must have once belonged to a man. Pete breaks
the kiss.

Come on. Let's get out of here. I've even got
moral or something. I don't even want to put my
hands on you in his house——

He sees Nancy across Temple's shoulder, and reacts.

Temple reacts to him, turns quickly, and sees Nancy too.
Nancy comes on into the room.

TEMPLE
(to Nancy)
What are you doing here?

NANCY
I brought my foot. So he can hold that cigarette
against it.

TEMPLE
So you're not just a thief: you're a spy too.

PETE
Maybe she's not a thief either. Maybe she brought
it back.
(they watch Nancy, who doesn't answer)
Or maybe she didn't. Maybe we had better use
that cigarette.
(to Nancy)
How about it? Is that what you came back for,
sure enough?

TEMPLE
(to Pete)
Hush. Take the bags and go on to the car.

PETE
(to Temple but watching Nancy)
I'll wait for you. There may be a little something
I can do here, after all.

TEMPLE
Go on, I tell you! Let's for God's sake get away
from here. Go on.

Pete watches Nancy for a moment longer, who stands facing them but not looking at anything, motionless, almost bemused, her face sad, brooding and inscrutable. Then Pete turns, goes to the table, picks up the lighter, seems about to pass on, then pauses again and with almost infinitesimal hesitation takes up the packet of letters, puts it back inside his coat, takes up the two packed bags and crosses to the french-window, passing Nancy, who is still looking at nothing and no one.

PETE
(to Nancy)
Not that I wouldn't like to, you know. For less than fifty bucks even. For old lang syne.

He transfers the bags to one hand, opens the french-window, starts to exit, pauses half-way out and looks back at Temple.

I'll be listening, in case you change your mind about the cigarette.

He goes on out, draws the door to after him. Just before it closes, Nancy speaks.

NANCY
Wait.

Pete stops, begins to open the door again.

TEMPLE
(quickly: to Pete)
Go on! Go on! For God's sake go on!

Pete exits, shuts the door after him. Nancy and Temple face each other.

NANCY
Maybe I was wrong to think that just hiding that

money and diamonds was going to stop you. Maybe I ought to have give it to him yesterday as soon as I found where you had hid it. Then wouldn't nobody between here and Chicago or Texas seen anything of him but his dust.

TEMPLE
So you did steal it. And you saw what good that did, didn't you?

NANCY
If you can call it stealing, then so can I. Because wasn't but part of it yours to begin with. Just the diamonds was yours. Not to mention that money is almost two thousand dollars, that you told me was just two hundred and that you told him was even less than that, just fifty. No wonder he wasn't worried—about just fifty dollars. He wouldn't even be worried if he knowed it was even the almost two thousand it is, let alone the two hundred you told me it was. He ain't even worried about whether or not you'll have any money at all when you get out to the car. He knows that all he's got to do is, just wait and keep his hand on you and maybe just mash hard enough with it, and you'll get another passel of money and diamonds too out of your husband or your pa. Only, this time he'll have his hand on you and you'll have a little trouble telling him it's just fifty dollars instead of almost two thousand——

Temple steps quickly forward and slaps Nancy across the face. Nancy steps back. As she does so, the packet of money and the jewel box fall to the floor from inside her

F

topcoat. Temple stops, looking down at the money and
jewels. Nancy recovers.

> Yes, there it is, that caused all the grief and ruin.
> If you hadn't been somebody that would have a
> box of diamonds and a husband that you could
> find almost two thousand dollars in his britches
> pocket while he was asleep, that man wouldn't
> have tried to sell you them letters. Maybe if I
> hadn't taken and hid it, you would have give it to
> him before you come to this. Or maybe if I had
> just give it to him yesterday and got the letters, or
> maybe if I was to take it out to where he's waiting
> in that car right now, and say, Here, man, take
> your money——

TEMPLE
Try it. Pick it up and take it out to him, and see.
If you'll wait until I finish packing, you can even
carry the bag.

NANCY
I know. It ain't even the letters any more. Maybe
it never was. It was already there in whoever could
write the kind of letters that even eight years afterward could still make grief and ruin. The letters
never did matter. You could have got them back
at any time; he even tried to give them to you
twice——

TEMPLE
How much spying have you been doing?

NANCY
All of it.—You wouldn't even needed money and

diamonds to get them back. A woman don't need it. All she needs is womanishness to get anything she wants from men. You could have done that right here in the house, without even tricking your husband into going off fishing.

TEMPLE

A perfect example of whore morality. But then, if I can say whore, so can you, can't you? Maybe the difference is, I decline to be one in my husband's house.

NANCY

I ain't talking about your husband. I ain't even talking about you. I'm talking about two little children.

TEMPLE

So am I. Why else do you think I sent Bucky on to his grandmother, except to get him out of a house where the man he has been taught to call his father, may at any moment decide to tell him he has none? As clever a spy as you must surely have heard my husband——

NANCY

(interrupts)

I've heard him. And I heard you too. You fought back—that time. Not for yourself, but for that little child. But now you have quit.

TEMPLE

Quit?

NANCY

Yes. You gave up. You gave up the child too. Willing to risk never seeing him again maybe.

(Temple doesn't answer)

That's right. You don't need to make no excuses to me. Just tell me what you must have already strengthened your mind up to telling all the rest of the folks that are going to ask you that. You are willing to risk it. Is that right?

(Temple doesn't answer)

All right. We'll say you have answered it. So that settles Bucky. Now answer me this one. Who are you going to leave the other one with?

TEMPLE

Leave her with? A six-months-old baby?

NANCY

That's right. Of course you can't leave her. Not with nobody. You can't no more leave a six-months-old baby with nobody while you run away from your husband with another man, than you can take a six-months-old baby with you on that trip. That's what I'm talking about. So maybe you'll just leave it in there in that cradle; it'll cry for a while, but it's too little to cry very loud and so maybe won't nobody hear it and come meddling, especially with the house shut up and locked until Mr. Gowan gets back next week, and probably by that time it will have hushed——

TEMPLE

Are you really trying to make me hit you again?

NANCY

Or maybe taking her with you will be just as easy, at least until the first time you write Mr. Gowan

or your pa for money and they don't send it as
quick as your new man thinks they ought to, and
he throws you and the baby both out. Then you
can drop it into a garbage can and no more
trouble to you or anybody, because then you will
be rid of both of them——
>   (Temple makes a convulsive movement,
>   then catches herself)

Hit me. Light you a cigarette too, I told you and
him both I brought my foot. Here it is.
>   (she raises her foot slightly)

I've tried everything else; I reckon I can try that
too.

TEMPLE
(repressed, furious)
Hush. I tell you for the last time. Hush.

NANCY
I've hushed.
She doesn't move. She is not looking at Temple. There is
a slight change in her voice or manner, though we only
realise later that she is not addressing Temple.
>   I've tried. I've tried everything I know. You can
>   see that.

TEMPLE
Which nobody will dispute. You threatened me
with my children, and even with my husband—
if you can call my husband a threat. You even
stole my elopement money. Oh yes, nobody will
dispute that you tried. Though at least you
brought the money back. Pick it up.

NANCY

You said you don't need it.

TEMPLE

I don't. Pick it up.

NANCY

No more do I need it.

TEMPLE

Pick it up, anyway. You can keep your next week's pay out of it when you give it back to Mr. Gowan.

Nancy stoops and gathers up the money, and gathers the jewellery back into its box, and puts them on the table.

(quieter)

Nancy.

(Nancy looks at her)

I'm sorry. Why do you force me to this—hitting and screaming at you, when you have always been so good to my children and me—my husband too —all of us—trying to hold us together in a household, a family, that anybody should have known all the time couldn't possibly hold together? even in decency, let alone happiness?

NANCY

I reckon I'm ignorant. I don't know that yet. Besides, I ain't talking about any household or happiness neither——

TEMPLE

(with sharp command)

Nancy!

NANCY

—I'm talking about two little children——

TEMPLE

I said, hush.

NANCY

I can't hush. I'm going to ask you one more time.
Are you going to do it?

TEMPLE

Yes!

NANCY

Maybe I am ignorant. You got to say it out in
words yourself, so I can hear them. Say, I'm
going to do it.

TEMPLE

You heard me. I'm going to do it.

NANCY

Money or no money.

TEMPLE

Money or no money.

NANCY

Children or no children.
    (Temple doesn't answer)
To leave one with a man that's willing to believe
the child ain't got no father, willing to take the
other one to a man that don't even want no
children——
    (They stare at one another)
If you can do it, you can say it.

TEMPLE

Yes! Children or no children! Now get out of here. Take your part of that money, and get out. Here——

Temple goes quickly to the table, removes two or three bills from the mass of banknotes, and hands them to Nancy, who takes them. Temple takes up the rest of the money, takes up her bag from the table and opens it. Nancy crosses quietly toward the nursery, picking up the milk bottle from the table as she passes, and goes on. With the open bag in one hand and the money in the other, Temple notices Nancy's movement.

What are you doing?

NANCY

(still moving)

This bottle has got cold. I'm going to warm it in the bathroom.

Then Nancy stops and looks back at Temple, with something so strange in her look that Temple, about to resume putting the money into the bag, pauses too, watching Nancy. When Nancy speaks, it is like the former speech: we don't realise until afterward what it signifies.

I tried everything I knowed. You can see that.

TEMPLE

(peremptory, commanding)

Nancy.

NANCY

(quietly, turning on)

I've hushed.

She exits through the door into the nursery. Temple

finishes putting the money into the bag, and closes it and puts it back on the table. Then she turns to the baby's bag. She tidies it, checks rapidly over its contents, takes up the jewel box and stows it in the bag and closes the bag. All this takes about two minutes; she has just closed the bag when Nancy emerges quietly from the nursery, without the milk bottle, and crosses, pausing at the table only long enough to put back on it the money Temple gave her, then starts toward the opposite door through which she first entered the room.

TEMPLE

Now what?
Nancy goes on toward the other door. Temple watches her.

Nancy.

    (Nancy pauses, still not looking back)
Don't think too hard of me.

    (Nancy waits, immobile, looking at
    nothing. When Temple doesn't con-
    tinue, she moves again toward the door)
If I—it ever comes up, I'll tell everybody you did your best. You tried. But you were right. It wasn't even the letters. It was me.

    (Nancy moves on)
Good-bye, Nancy.

    (Nancy reaches the door)
You've got your key. I'll leave your money here on the table. You can get it——

    (Nancy exits)
Nancy!
There is no answer. Temple looks a moment longer at

the empty door, shrugs, moves, takes up the money Nancy left, glances about, crosses to the littered desk and takes up a paperweight and returns to the table and puts the money beneath the weight; now moving rapidly and with determination, she takes up the blanket from the table and crosses to the nursery door and exits through it. A second or two, then she screams. The lights flicker and begin to dim, fade swiftly into complete darkness, over the scream.

The stage is in complete darkness.

Same as Scene I. Governor's Office. 3.09 A.M. March
  twelfth.

The lights go on upper left. The scene is the same as
before, Scene I, except that Gowan Stevens now sits in
the chair behind the desk where the Governor had been
sitting and the Governor is no longer in the room.
Temple now kneels before the desk, facing it, her arms on
the desk and her face buried in her arms. Stevens now
stands beside and over her. The hands of the clock show
nine minutes past three.

Temple does not know that the Governor has gone and
that her husband is now in the room.

> TEMPLE
> (her face still hidden)
> And that's all. The police came, and the murderess
> still sitting in a chair in the kitchen in the dark,
> saying 'Yes, Lord, I done it,' and then in the cell
> at the jail still saying it——
>> (Stevens leans and touches her arm, as if
>> to help her up. She resists, though still
>> not raising her head)
> Not yet. It's my cue to stay down here until
> his honour or excellency grants our plea, isn't it?
> Or have I already missed my cue forever even
> if the sovereign state should offer me a hand-
> kerchief right out of its own elected public suffrage
> dressing-gown pocket? Because see?

> (she raises her face, quite blindly, tearless,
> still not looking toward the chair where
> she could see Gowan instead of the
> Governor, into the full glare of the light)

Still no tears.

STEVENS

Get up, Temple.

> (he starts to lift her again, but before he
> can do so, she rises herself, standing, her
> face still turned away from the desk, still
> blind; she puts her arm up almost in the
> gesture of a little girl about to cry, but
> instead she merely shields her eyes from
> the light while her pupils re-adjust)

TEMPLE

Nor cigarette either; this time it certainly won't
take long, since all he has to say is, No.

> . (still not turning her face to look, even
> though she is now speaking directly to
> the Governor who she still thinks is
> sitting behind the desk)

Because you aren't going to save her, are you?
Because all this was not for the sake of her soul
because her soul doesn't need it, but for mine.

STEVENS

> (gently)

Why not finish first? Tell the rest of it. You had
started to say something about the jail.

TEMPLE

The jail. They had the funeral the next day—

Gowan had barely reached New Orleans, so he chartered an aeroplane back that morning—and in Jefferson, everything going to the graveyard passes the jail, or going anywhere else for that matter, passing right under the upstairs barred windows —the bullpen and the cells where the Negro prisoners—the crapshooters and whiskey-pedlars and vagrants and the murderers and murderesses too—can look down and enjoy it, enjoy the funerals too. Like this. Some white person you know is in a jail or a hospital, and right off you say, How ghastly: not at the shame or the pain, but the walls, the locks, and before you even know it, you have sent them books to read, cards, puzzles to play with. But not Negroes. You don't even think about the cards and puzzles and books. And so all of a sudden you find out with a kind of terror, that they have not only escaped having to read, they have escaped having to escape. So whenever you pass the jail, you can see them— no, not them, you don't see them at all, you just see the hands among the bars of the windows, not tapping or fidgeting or even holding, gripping the bars like white hands would be, but just lying there among the interstices, not just at rest, but even restful, already shaped and easy and un- anguished to the handles of the ploughs and axes and hoes, and the mops and brooms and the rockers of white folks' cradles, until even the steel bars fitted them too without alarm or anguish. You see? not gnarled and twisted with work at all, but even limbered and suppled by it, smoothed and even softened, as though with only the penny-change of simple sweat they had already got the same thing the white ones have to pay dollars by the ounce jar for. Not immune to work, and in compromise with work is not the right word either, but in confederacy with work and so free from it; in armistice, peace;—the same long supple hands serene and immune to anguish, so that all the owners of them need to look out with, to see with —to look out at the outdoors—the funerals, the passing, the people, the freedom, the sunlight, the free air—are just the hands: not the eyes: just the hands lying there among the bars and looking out, that can see the shape of the plough or hoe or axe before daylight comes; and even in the dark, without even having to turn on the light, can not only find the child, the baby—not her child but yours, the white one—but the trouble and discomfort too —the hunger, the wet nappie, the unfastened safety-pin—and see to remedy it. You see. If I could just cry. There was another one, a man this time, before my time in Jefferson but Uncle Gavin will remember this too. His wife had just died— they had been married only two weeks—and he buried her and so at first he tried just walking the country roads at night for exhaustion and sleep, only that failed and then he tried getting drunk so he could sleep, and that failed and then he tried fighting and then he cut a white man's throat with a razor in a dice game and so at last he could sleep for a little while; which was where the sheriff found him, asleep on the wooden floor of the

gallery of the house he had rented for his wife, his
marriage, his life, his old age. Only that waked
him up, and so in the jail that afternoon, all of a
sudden it took the jailer and a deputy and five
other Negro prisoners just to throw him down and
hold him while they locked the chains on him—
lying there on the floor with more than a half-
dozen men panting to hold him down, and what
do you think he said? 'Look like I just can't quit
thinking. Look like I just can't quit.'

> (she ceases, blinking, rubs her eyes and
> then extends one hand blindly toward
> Stevens, who has already shaken out his
> handkerchief and hands it to her. There
> are still no tears on her face; she merely
> takes the handkerchief and dabs, pats at
> her eyes with it as if it were a powder-
> puff, talking again)

But we have passed the jail, haven't we? We're in
the Courtroom now. It was the same there; Uncle
Gavin had rehearsed her, of course, which was
easy, since all you can say when they ask you to
answer to a murder charge is, Not Guilty. Otherwise, they can't even have a trial; they would have
to hurry out and find another murderer before
they could take the next official step. So they asked
her, all correct and formal among the judges and
lawyers and bailiffs and jury and the Scales and the
Sword and the flag and the ghosts of Coke upon
Littleton upon Bonaparte and Julius Cæsar and all
the rest of it, not to mention the eyes and the faces
which were getting a moving-picture show for

free since they had already paid for it in the taxes, and nobody really listening since there was only one thing she could say. Except that she didn't say it: just raising her head enough to be heard plain—not loud: just plain—and said, 'Guilty, Lord'—like that, disrupting and confounding and dispersing and flinging back two thousand years, the whole edifice of *corpus juris* and rules of evidence we have been working to make stand up by itself ever since Cæsar, like when without even watching yourself or even knowing you were doing it, you would reach out your hand and turn over a chip and expose to air and light and vision the frantic and aghast turmoil of an ant-hill. And moved the chip again, when even the ants must have thought there couldn't be another one within her reach: when they finally explained to her that to say she was not guilty, had nothing to do with truth but only with law, and this time she said it right, Not Guilty, and so then the jury could tell her she lied and everything was all correct again and, as everybody thought, even safe, since now she wouldn't be asked to say anything at all any more. Only, they were wrong; the jury said Guilty and the judge said Hang and now everybody was already picking up his hat to go home, when she picked up that chip too: the judge said, 'And may God have mercy on your soul,' and Nancy answered: 'Yes, Lord.'

> (she turns suddenly, almost briskly, speaking so briskly that her momentum carries her on past the instant when she

> sees and recognises Gowan sitting where
> she had thought all the time that the
> Governor was sitting and listening to her)

And that is all, this time. And so now you can tell
us. I know you're not going to save her, but now
you can say so. It won't be difficult. Just one
word——

> (she stops, arrested, utterly motionless,
> but even then she is first to recover)

Oh God.

> (Gowan rises quickly, Temple whirls to
> Stevens)

Why is it you must always believe in plants? Do
you have to? Is it because you have to? Because
you are a lawyer? No, I'm wrong. I'm sorry; I
was the one that started us hiding gimmicks on
each other, wasn't it?

> (quickly: turning to Gowan)

Of course; you didn't take the sleeping pill at all.
Which means you didn't even need to come here
for the Governor to hide you behind the door or
under the desk or wherever it was he was trying
to tell me you were hiding and listening, because
after all the Governor of a Southern state has got
to try to act like he regrets having to aberrate
from being a gentleman——

STEVENS
> (to Temple)

Stop it.

GOWAN
Maybe we both didn't start hiding soon enough—

by about eight years—not in desk drawers either,
but in two abandoned mine shafts, one in Siberia
and the other at the South Pole, maybe.

TEMPLE

All right. I didn't mean hiding. I'm sorry.

GOWAN

Don't be. Just draw on your eight years' interest
for that.
(to Stevens)
All right, all right; tell me to shut up too.
(to no one directly)
In fact, this may be the time for me to start
saying sorry for the next eight-year term. Just
give me a little time. Eight years of gratitude
might be a habit a little hard to break. So here
goes.
(to Temple)
I'm sorry. Forget it.

TEMPLE

I would have told you.

GOWAN

You did. Forget it. You see how easy it is? You
could have been doing that yourself for eight
years: every time I would say 'Say sorry, please,'
all you would need would be to answer: 'I did.
Forget it.'
(to Stevens)
I guess that's all, isn't it? We can go home
now.

(he starts to come around the desk)

TEMPLE

Wait.

> (Gowan stops; they look at each other)

Where are you going?

GOWAN

I said home, didn't I? To pick up Bucky and carry
him back to his own bed again.

> (they look at one another)

You're not even going to ask me where he is now?

> (answers himself)

Where we always leave our children when the
clutch——

STEVENS

> (to Gowan)

Maybe I will say shut up this time.

GOWAN

Only let me finish first. I was going to say, 'with
our handiest kinfolks.'

> (to Temple)

I carried him to Maggie's.

STEVENS

> (moving)

I think we can all go now. Come on.

GOWAN

So do I.

> (he comes on around the desk, and stops
> again; to Temple)

Make up your mind. Do you want to ride with
me, or Gavin?

STEVENS
(to Gowan)
Go on. You can pick up Bucky.

GOWAN
Right.
(he turns, starts toward the steps front,
where Temple and Stevens entered, then
stops)
That's right. I'm probably still supposed to use
the spy's entrance.
(he turns back, starts around the desk
again, toward the door at rear, sees
Temple's gloves and bag on the desk, and
takes them up and holds them out to her:
roughly almost)
Here. This is what they call evidence; don't forget
these.
(Temple takes the bag and gloves)
Gowan goes on toward the door at rear.

TEMPLE
(after him)
Did you have a hat and coat?
(he doesn't answer. He goes on, exits)
Oh, God. Again.

STEVENS
(touches her arm)
Come on.

TEMPLE
(not moving yet)
Tomorrow and tomorrow and tomorrow——

STEVENS

(speaking her thought, finishing the
sentence)

—he will wreck the car again against the wrong
tree, in the wrong place, and you will have to forgive him again, for the next eight years until he
can wreck the car again in the wrong place, against
the wrong tree——

TEMPLE

I was driving it too. I was driving some of the
time too.

STEVENS

(gently)

Then let that comfort you.

(he takes her arm again, turns her toward
the stairs)

Come on. It's late.

TEMPLE

(holds back)

Wait. He said, No.

STEVENS

Yes.

TEMPLE

Did he say why?

STEVENS

Yes. He can't.

TEMPLE

Can't? The Governor of a state, with all the legal
power to pardon or at least reprieve, can't?

STEVENS

That's just law. If it was only law, I could have
pleaded insanity for her at any time, without bringing you here at two o'clock in the morning——

TEMPLE

And the other parent too; don't forget that. I
don't know yet how you did it. . . . Yes, Gowan
was here first; he was just pretending to be asleep
when I carried Bucky in and put him in his bed;
yes, that was what you called that leaking valve,
when we stopped at the filling station to change
the wheel: to let him get ahead of us——

STEVENS

All right. He wasn't even talking about justice.
He was talking about a child, a little boy——

TEMPLE

That's right. Make it good: the same little boy to
hold whose normal and natural home together,
the murderess, the nigger, the dope-fiend whore,
didn't hesitate to cast the last gambit—and maybe
that's the wrong word too, isn't it?—she knew and
had: her own debased and worthless life. Oh yes, I
know that answer too; that was brought out here
tonight too: that a little child shall not suffer in
order to come unto Me. So good can come out
of evil.

STEVENS

It not only can, it must.

TEMPLE

So *touché*, then. Because what kind of natural and

normal home can that little boy have where his
father may at any time tell him he has no father?

STEVENS

Haven't you been answering that question every
day for six years? Didn't Nancy answer it for you
when she told you how you had fought back, not
for yourself, but for that little boy? Not to show
the father that he was wrong, nor even to prove
to the little boy that the father was wrong, but
to let the little boy learn with his own eyes that
nothing, not even that, which could possibly enter
that house, could ever harm him?

TEMPLE

But I quit. Nancy told you that too.

STEVENS

She doesn't think so now. Isn't that what she's
going to prove Friday morning?

TEMPLE

Friday. The black day. The day you never start on
a journey. Except that Nancy's journey didn't start
at daylight or sun-up or whenever it is polite and
tactful to hang people, day after tomorrow. Her
journey started that morning eight years ago when
I got on the train at the University——
      (she stops: a moment; then quietly)
Oh God, that was Friday too; that baseball game
was Friday——
      (rapidly)
You see? Don't you see? It's nowhere near enough
yet. Of course he wouldn't save her. If he did that,

it would be over: Gowan could just throw me out, which he may do yet, or I could throw Gowan out, which I could have done until it got too late now, too late forever now, or the judge could have thrown us both out and given Bucky to an orphanage, and it would be all over. But now it can go on, tomorrow and tomorrow and to-morrow, forever and forever and forever——

STEVENS
(gently tries to start her)
Come on.

TEMPLE
(holding back)
Tell me exactly what he did say. Not tonight: it couldn't have been tonight—or did he say it over the telephone, and we didn't even need——

STEVENS
He said it a week ago——

TEMPLE
Yes, about the same time when you sent the wire. What did he say?

STEVENS
(quotes)
'Who am I, to have the brazen temerity and hardi-hood to set the puny appanage of my office in the balance against that simple undeviable aim? Who am I, to render null and abrogate the purchase she made with that poor crazed lost and worthless life?'

TEMPLE
(wildly)

And good too—good and mellow too. So it was not even in hopes of saving her life, that I came here at two o'clock in the morning. It wasn't even to be told that he had already decided not to save her. It was not even to confess to my husband, but to do it in the hearing of two strangers, something which I had spent eight years trying to expiate so that my husband wouldn't have to know about it. Don't you see? That's just suffering. Not for anything: just suffering.

STEVENS

You came here to affirm the very thing which Nancy is going to die tomorrow morning to postulate: that little children, as long as they are little children, shall be intact, unanguished, untorn, unterrified.

TEMPLE
(quietly)

All right. I have done that. Can we go home now?

STEVENS

Yes.

> (she turns, moves toward the steps, Stevens beside her. As she reaches the first step, she falters, seems to stumble slightly, like a sleepwalker. Stevens steadies her, but at once she frees her arm, and begins to descend)

TEMPLE

(on the first step: to no one, still with
that sleepwalker air)

To save my soul—if I have a soul. If there is a
God to save it—a God who wants it——

(CURTAIN)

ACT THREE

THE JAIL (Nor Even Yet Quite Relinquish——)

So, although in a sense the jail was both older and less old than the courthouse, in actuality, in time, in observation and memory, it was older even than the town itself. Because there was no town until there was a courthouse, and no courthouse until (like some insentient unweaned creature torn violently from the dug of its dam) the floorless lean-to rabbit-hutch housing the iron chest was reft from the log flank of the jail and transmogrified into a by-neo-Greek-out-of-Georgian-England edifice set in the centre of what in time would be the town Square (as a result of which, the town itself had moved one block south—or rather, no town then and yet, the courthouse itself the catalyst: a mere dusty widening of the trace, trail, pathway in a forest of oak and ash and hickory and sycamore and flowering catalpa and dogwood and judas tree and persimmon and wild plum, with on one side old Alec Holston's tavern and coaching-yard, and a little farther along, Ratcliffe's trading-post-store and the blacksmith's, and diagonal to all of them, *en face* and solitary beyond the dust, the log jail; moved—the town—complete and intact, one block southward, so that now, a century and a quarter later, the coaching-yard and Ratcliffe's store were gone and old Alec's tavern and the blacksmith's were a hotel and a garage, on a main thoroughfare true enough but still a business side-street, and the jail across from them, though transformed also now into two storeys of Georgian brick by the hand [or anyway pocket-books] of Sartoris and Sutpen and Louis

187

Grenier, faced not even on a side-street but on an alley);

And so, being older than all, it had seen all: the mutation and the change: and, in that sense, had recorded them (indeed, as Gavin Stevens, the town lawyer and the county amateur Cincinnatus, was wont to say, if you would peruse in unbroken—aye, overlapping—continuity the history of a community, look not in the church registers and the courthouse records, but beneath the successive layers of calsomine and creosote and white-wash on the walls of the jail, since only in that forcible carceration does man find the idleness in which to compose, in the gross and simple terms of his gross and simple lusts and yearnings, the gross and simple recapitulations of his gross and simple heart); invisible and impacted, not only beneath the annual inside creosote-and-whitewash of bullpen and cell, but on the blind outside walls too, first the simple mud-chinked log ones and then the symmetric brick, not only the scrawled illiterate repetitive unimaginative doggerel and the perspectiveless almost prehistoric sexual picture-writing, but the images, the panorama not only of the town but of its days and years until a century and better had been accomplished, filled not only with its mutation and change from a halting-place: to a community: to a settlement: to a village: to a town, but with the shapes and motions, the gestures of passion and hope and travail and endurance, of the men and women and children in their successive overlapping generations long after the subjects which had reflected the images were vanished and replaced and again re-placed, as when you stand say alone in a dim and empty

room and believe, hypnotised beneath the vast weight of
man's incredible and enduring *Was*, that perhaps by turning your head aside you will see from the corner of your
eye the turn of a moving limb—a gleam of crinoline, a
laced wrist, perhaps even a Cavalier plume—who knows?
provided there is will enough, perhaps even the face
itself three hundred years after it was dust—the eyes, two
jellied tears filled with arrogance and pride and satiety
and knowledge of anguish and foreknowledge of death,
saying no to death across twelve generations, asking still
the old same unanswerable question three centuries after
that which reflected them had learned that the answer
didn't matter, or—better still—had forgotten the asking
of it—in the shadowy fathomless dreamlike depths of an
old mirror which has looked at too much too long;

But not in shadow, not this one, this mirror, these logs:
squatting in the full glare of the stump-pocked clearing
during those first summers, solitary on its side of the
dusty widening marked with an occasional wheel but
mostly by the prints of horses and men: Pettigrew's
private pony express until he and it were replaced by a
monthly stagecoach from Memphis, the race horse which
Jason Compson traded to Ikkemotubbe, old Mohataha's
son and the last ruling Chickasaw chief in that section, for
a square of land so large that, as the first formal survey
revealed, the new courthouse would have been only
another of Compson's outbuildings had not the town
Corporation bought enough of it (at Compson's price)
to forefend themselves being trespassers, and the saddle-
mare which bore Doctor Habersham's worn black bag
(and which drew the buggy after Doctor Habersham got

too old and stiff to mount the saddle), and the mules
which drew the wagon in which, seated in a rocking chair
beneath a French parasol held by a Negro slave girl, old
Mohataha would come to town on Saturdays (and came
that last time to set her capital X on the paper which
ratified the dispossession of her people forever, coming
in the wagon that time too, barefoot as always but in
the purple silk dress which her son, Ikkemotubbe, had
brought her back from France, and a hat crowned with
the royal-coloured plume of a queen, beneath the slave-
held parasol still and with another female slave child
squatting on her other side holding the crusted slippers
which she had never been able to get her feet into, and
in the back of the wagon the petty rest of the unmarked
Empire flotsam her son had brought to her which was
small enough to be moved; driving for the last time out
of the woods into the dusty widening before Ratcliffe's
store where the Federal land agent and his marshal waited
for her with the paper, and stopped the mules and sat for
a little time, the young men of her bodyguard squatting
quietly about the halted wagon after the eight-mile walk,
while from the gallery of the store and of Holston's
tavern the settlement—the Ratcliffes and Compsons and
Peabodys and Pettigrews [not Grenier and Holston and
Habersham, because Louis Grenier declined to come in to
see it, and for the same reason old Alec Holston sat alone
on that hot afternoon before the smouldering log in the
fireplace of his taproom, and Doctor Habersham was
dead and his son had already departed for the West with
his bride, who was Mohataha's granddaughter, and his
father-in-law, Mohataha's son, Ikkemotubbe]—looked
on, watched: the inscrutable ageless wrinkled face, the fat

shapeless body dressed in the cast-off garments of a French queen, which on her looked like the Sunday costume of the madam of a rich Natchez or New Orleans brothel, sitting in a battered wagon inside a squatting ring of her household troops, her young men dressed in their Sunday clothes for travelling too: then she said, 'Where is this Indian territory?' And they told her: West. 'Turn the mules west,' she said, and someone did so, and she took the pen from the agent and made her X on the paper and handed the pen back and the wagon moved, the young men rising too, and she vanished so across that summer afternoon to that terrific and infinitesimal creak and creep of ungreased wheels, herself immobile beneath the rigid parasol, grotesque and regal, bizarre and moribund, like obsolescence's self riding off the stage its own obsolete catafalque, looking not once back, not once back toward home);

But most of all, the prints of men—the fitted shoes which Doctor Habersham and Louis Grenier had brought from the Atlantic seaboard, the cavalry boots in which Alec Holston had ridden behind Francis Marion, and—more myriad almost than leaves, outnumbering all the others lumped together—the moccasins, the deerhide sandals of the forest, worn not by the Indians but by white men, the pioneers, the long hunters, as though they had not only vanquished the wilderness but had even stepped into the very footgear of them they dispossessed (and mete and fitting so, since it was by means of his feet and legs that the white man conquered America; the closed and split U's of his horses and cattle overlay his own prints always, merely consolidating his victory);—(the jail)

watched them all, red men and white and black—the
pioneers, the hunters, the forest men with rifles, who
made the same light rapid soundless toed-in almost heel-
less prints as the red men they dispossessed and who in
fact dispossessed the red men for that reason: not because
of the grooved barrel but because they could enter the
red man's milieu and make the same footprints that he
made; the husbandman printing deep the hard heels of his
brogans because of the weight he bore on his shoulders:
axe and saw and plough-stock, who dispossessed the
forest man for the obverse reason: because with his saw
and axe he simply removed, obliterated, the milieu in
which alone the forest man could exist; then the land
speculators and the traders in slaves and whiskey who
followed the husbandmen, and the politicians who followed the land speculators, printing deeper and deeper
the dust of that dusty widening, until at last there was no
mark of Chickasaw left in it any more; watching (the
jail) them all, from the first innocent days when Doctor
Habersham and his son and Alex Holston and Louis
Grenier were first guests and then friends of Ikkemotubbe's Chickasaw clan; then an Indian agent and a land-
office and a trading-post, and suddenly Ikkemotubbe and
his Chickasaws were themselves the guests without being
friends of the Federal Government; then Ratcliffe, and
the trading-post was no longer simply an Indian trading-
post, though Indians were still welcome, of course (since,
after all, they owned the land or anyway were on it first
and claimed it), then Compson with his race horse and
presently Compson began to own the Indian accounts for
tobacco and calico and jeans pants and cooking-pots on
Ratcliffe's books (in time he would own Ratcliffe's books

too) and one day Ikkemotubbe owned the race horse and
Compson owned the land itself, some of which the city
fathers would have to buy from him at his price in order
to establish a town; and Pettigrew with his tri-weekly
mail, and then a monthly stage and the new faces coming
in faster than old Alex Holston, arthritic and irascible,
hunkered like an old surly bear over his smouldering
hearth even in the heat of summer (he alone now of that
original three, since old Grenier no longer came in to the
settlement, and old Doctor Habersham was dead, and the
old doctor's son, in the opinion of the settlement, had
already turned Indian and renegade even at the age of
twelve or fourteen) any longer made any effort, wanted,
to associate names with; and now indeed the last moccasin
print vanished from that dusty widening, the last toed-in
heel-less light soft quick long-striding print pointing west
for an instant, then trodden from the sight and memory
of man by a heavy leather heel engaged not in the traffic
of endurance and hardihood and survival, but in money
—taking with it (the print) not only the moccasins but
the deer-hide leggings and jerkin too, because Ikkemotubbe's Chickasaws now wore Eastern factory-made
jeans and shoes sold them on credit out of Ratcliffe's and
Compson's general store, walking in to the settlement on
the white man's Saturday, carrying the alien shoes rolled
neatly in the alien pants under their arms, to stop at the
bridge over Compson's creek long enough to bathe their
legs and feet before donning the pants and shoes, then
coming on to squat all day on the store gallery eating
cheese and crackers and peppermint candy (bought on
credit too out of Compson's and Ratcliffe's showcase)
and now not only they but Habersham and Holston and

G

Grenier too were there on sufferance, anachronistic and alien, not really an annoyance yet but simply a discomfort;

Then they were gone; the jail watched that: the halted ungreased unpainted wagon, the span of underfed mules attached to it by fragments of Eastern harness supplemented by raw deer-hide thongs, the nine young men— the wild men, tameless and proud, who even in their own generation's memory had been free and, in that of their fathers, the heirs of kings—squatting about it, waiting, quiet and composed, not even dressed in the ancient forest-softened deerskins of their freedom but in the formal regalia of the white man's inexplicable ritualistic sabbaticals: broadcloth trousers and white shirts with boiled-starch bosoms (because they were travelling now; they would be visible to outworld, to strangers:—and carrying the New England-made shoes under their arms too since the distance would be long and walking was better barefoot), the shirts collarless and cravatless true enough and with the tails worn outside, but still board-rigid, gleaming, pristine, and in the rocking chair in the wagon, beneath the slave-borne parasol, the fat shapeless old matriarch in the regal sweat-stained purple silk and the plumed hat, barefoot too of course but, being a queen, with another slave to carry her slippers, putting her cross to the paper and then driving on, vanishing slowly and terrifically to the slow and terrific creak and squeak of the ungreased wagon—apparently and apparently only, since in reality it was as though, instead of putting an inked cross at the foot of a sheet of paper, she had lighted the train of a mine set beneath a dam, a dyke, a barrier already straining, bulging, bellying, not

only towering over the land but leaning, looming, imminent with collapse, so that it only required the single light
touch of the pen in that brown illiterate hand, and the
wagon did not vanish slowly and terrifically from the
scene to the terrific sound of its ungreased wheels, but
was swept, hurled, flung not only out of Yoknapatawpha
County and Mississippi but the United States too, immobile and intact—the wagon, the mules, the rigid shapeless
old Indian woman and the nine heads which surrounded
her—like a float or a piece of stage property dragged
rapidly into the wings across the very backdrop and amid
the very hustle of the property-men setting up for the
next scene and act before the curtain had even had time
to fall;

There was no time; the next act and scene itself clearing its own stage without waiting for property-men; or
rather, not even bothering to clear the stage but com-
mencing the new act and scene right in the midst of the
phantoms, the fading wraiths of that old time which had
been exhausted, used up, to be no more and never return: as though the mere and simple orderly ordinary
succession of days was not big enough, comprised not
scope enough, and so weeks and months and years had to
be condensed and compounded into one burst, one surge,
one soundless roar filled with one word: town: city: with
a name: Jefferson; men's mouths and their incredulous
faces (faces to which old Alex Holston had long since
ceased trying to give names or, for that matter, even to
recognise) were filled with it; that was only yesterday,
and by tomorrow the vast bright rush and roar had swept
the very town one block south, leaving in the tideless

backwater of an alley on a side-street the old jail which, like the old mirror, had already looked at too much too long, or like the patriarch who, whether or not he decreed the conversion of the mud-chinked cabin into a mansion, had at least foreseen it, is now not only content but even prefers the old chair on the back gallery, free of the rustle of blueprints and the uproar of bickering architects in the already dismantled living-room;

It (the old jail) didn't care, tideless in that backwash, in- sulated by that city block of space from the turmoil of the town's birthing, the mud-chinked log walls even car- cerant of the flotsam of an older time already on its rapid way out too: an occasional runaway slave or drunken Indian or shoddy would-be heir of the old tradition of Mason or Hare or Harpe (biding its time until, the court- house finished, the jail too would be translated into brick, but, unlike the courthouse, merely a veneer of brick, the old mud-chinked logs of the ground floor still intact behind the patterned and symmetric sheath); no longer even watching now, merely cognisant, remembering: only yesterday was a wilderness ordinary, a store, a smithy, and already today was not a town, a city, but the town and city: named; not a courthouse but *the* court- house, rising surging like the fixed blast of a rocket, not even finished yet but already looming, beacon focus and lodestar, already taller than anything else, out of the rapid and fading wilderness—not the wilderness receding from the rich and arable fields as tide recedes, but rather the fields themselves, rich and inexhaustible to the plough, rising sunward and airward out of swamp and morass, themselves thrusting back and down brake and thicket,

bayou and bottom and forest, along with the copeless
denizens—the wild men and animals—which once haunted
them, wanting, dreaming, imagining, no other—lodestar
and pole, drawing the people—the men and women and
children, the maidens, the marriageable girls and the
young men, flowing, pouring in with their tools and
goods and cattle and slaves and gold money, behind ox-
or mule-teams, by steam-boat up Ikkemotubbe's old
river from the Mississippi; only yesterday Pettigrew's
pony express had been displaced by a stage-coach, yet
already there was talk of a railroad less than a hundred
miles to the north, to run all the way from Memphis to
the Atlantic Ocean;

Going fast now: only seven years, and not only was the
courthouse finished, but the jail too: not a new jail of
course but the old one veneered over with brick, into two
storeys, with white trim and iron-barred windows: only
its face lifted, because behind the veneer were still the old
ineradicable bones, the old ineradicable remembering: the
old logs immured intact and lightless between the tiered
symmetric bricks and the whitewashed plaster, immune
now even to having to look, see, watch that new time
which in a few years more would not even remember
that the old logs were there behind the brick or had ever
been, an age from which the drunken Indian had vanished,
leaving only the highwayman, who had wagered his
liberty on his luck, and the runaway nigger who, having
no freedom to stake, had wagered merely his milieu; that
rapid, that fast: Sutpen's untamable Paris architect long
since departed, vanished (one hoped) back to wherever it
was he had made that aborted midnight try to regain and

had been overtaken and caught in the swamp, not (as the town knew now) by Sutpen and Sutpen's wild West Indian headman and Sutpen's bear hounds, nor even by Sutpen's destiny nor even by his (the architect's) own, but by that of the town: the long invincible arm of Progress itself reaching into that midnight swamp to pluck him out of that bayed circle of dogs and naked Negroes and pine torches, and stamped the town with him like a rubber signature and then released him, not flung him away like a squeezed-out tube of paint, but rather (inattentive too) merely opening its fingers, its hand; stamping his (the architect's) imprint not on just the courthouse and the jail, but on the whole town, the flow and trickle of his bricks never even faltering, his moulds and kilns building the two churches and then that Female Academy a certificate from which, to a young woman of North Mississippi or West Tennessee, would presently have the same mystic significance as an invitation dated from Windsor Castle and signed by Queen Victoria would for a young female from Long Island or Philadelphia;

That fast now: tomorrow, and the railroad did run unbroken from Memphis to Carolina, the light-wheeled bulb-stacked wood-burning engines shrieking among the swamps and cane-brakes where bear and panther still lurked, and through the open woods where browsing deer still drifted in pale bands like unwinded smoke: because they—the wild animals, the beasts—remained, they coped, they would endure; a day, and they would flee, lumber, scuttle across the clearings already overtaken and relinquished by the hawk-shaped shadows of mail planes; they would endure, only the wild men were

gone; indeed, tomorrow, and there would be grown men
in Jefferson who could not even remember a drunken
Indian in the jail; another tomorrow—so quick, so rapid,
so fast—and not even a highwayman any more of the old
true sanguinary girt and tradition of Hare and Mason and
the mad Harpes; even Murrell, their thrice-compounded
heir and apotheosis, who had taken his heritage of simple
rapacity and bloodlust and converted it into a bloody
dream of outlaw-empire, was gone, finished, as obsolete
as Alexander, checkmated and stripped not even by man
but by Progress, by a pierceless front of middle-class
morality, which refused him even the dignity of execution as a felon, but instead merely branded him on the
hand like an Elizabethan pickpocket—until all that remained of the old days for the jail to incarcerate was the
runaway slave, for his little hour more, his little minute
yet while the time, the land, the nation, the American
earth, whirled faster and faster toward the plunging
precipice of its destiny;

That fast, that rapid: a commodity in the land now which
until now had dealt first in Indians: then in acres and
sections and boundaries:—an economy: Cotton: a king:
omnipotent and omnipresent: a destiny of which (obvious
now) the plough and the axe had been merely the tools;
not plough and axe which had effaced the wilderness, but
Cotton: petty globules of Motion weightless and myriad
even in the hand of a child, incapable even of wadding a
rifle, let alone of charging it, yet potent enough to sever
the very taproots of oak and hickory and gum, leaving
the acre-shading tops to wither and vanish in one single
season beneath that fierce minted glare; not the rifle nor

the plough which drove at last the bear and deer and
panther into the last jungle fastnesses of the river bottoms,
but Cotton; not the soaring cupola of the courthouse
drawing people into the country, but that same white tide
sweeping them in: that tender skim covering the winter's
brown earth, burgeoning through spring and summer
into September's white surf crashing against the flanks of
gin and warehouse and ringing like bells on the marble
counters of the banks: altering not just the face of the
land, but the complexion of the town too, creating its
own parasitic aristocracy not only behind the columned
porticoes of the plantation houses, but in the counting-
rooms of merchants and bankers and the sanctums of
lawyers, and not only these last, but finally nadir complete: the county offices too: of sheriff and tax-collector
and bailiff and turnkey and clerk; doing overnight to the
old jail what Sutpen's architect with all his brick and iron
smithwork, had not been able to accomplish—the old jail
which had been unavoidable, a necessity, like a public
convenience, and which, like the public convenience, was
not ignored but simply by mutual concord, not seen, not
looked at, not named by its purpose and aim, yet which
to the older people of the town, in spite of Sutpen's
architect's face-lifting, was still the old jail—now translated into an integer, a movable pawn on the county's
political board like the sheriff's star or the clerk's bond
or the bailiff's wand of office; converted indeed now,
elevated (an apotheosis) ten feet above the level of the
town, so that the old buried log walls now contained the
living-quarters for the turnkey's family and the kitchen
from which his wife catered, at so much a meal, to the
city's and the county's prisoners—perquisite not for work

or capability for work, but for political fidelity and the numerality of votable kin by blood or marriage—a jailor or turnkey, himself someone's cousin and with enough other cousins and in-laws of his own to have assured the election of sheriff or chancery- or circuit-clerk—a failed farmer who was not at all the victim of his time but, on the contrary, was its master, since his inherited and inescapable incapacity to support his family by his own efforts had matched him with an era and a land where government was founded on the working premise of being primarily an asylum for ineptitude and indigence, for the private business failures among your or your wife's kin whom otherwise you yourself would have to support—so much his destiny's master that, in a land and time where a man's survival depended not only on his ability to drive a straight furrow and to fell a tree without maiming or destroying himself, that fate had supplied to him one child: a frail anæmic girl with narrow workless hands lacking even the strength to milk a cow, and then capped its own vanquishment and eternal subjugation by the paradox of giving him for his patronymic the designation of the vocation at which he was to fail: Farmer; this was the incumbent, the turnkey, the jailor; the old tough logs which had known Ikkemotubbe's drunken Chickasaws and brawling teamsters and trappers and flatboatmen (and—for that one short summer night—the four highwaymen, one of whom might have been the murderer, Wiley Harpe), were now the bower framing a window in which mused hour after hour and day and month and year, the frail blonde girl not only incapable of (or at least excused from) helping her mother cook, but even of drying the dishes after her mother (or father perhaps) washed them—musing, not even waiting for anyone or anything, as far as the town knew, not even pensive, as far as the town knew: just musing amid her blonde hair in the window facing the country town street, day after day, and month after month and—as the town remembered it—year after year for what must have been three or four of them, inscribing at some moment the fragile and indelible signature of her meditation in one of the panes of it (the window): her frail and workless name, scratched by a diamond ring in her frail and work-less hand, and the date: *Cecilia Farmer April 16th 1861;*

At which moment the destiny of the land, the nation, the South, the state, the county, was already whirling into the plunge of its precipice, not that the state and the South knew it, because the first seconds of fall always seem like soar: a weightless deliberation preliminary to a rush not downward but upward, the falling body reversed during that second by transubstantiation into the upward rush of earth; a soar, an apex, the South's own apotheosis of its destiny and its pride, Mississippi and Yoknapatawpha County not last in this, Mississippi among the first of the eleven to ratify secession, the regiment of infantry which John Sartoris raised and organised with Jefferson for its headquarters, going to Virginia numbered Two in the roster of Mississippi regiments, the jail watching that too but just by cognisance from a block away: that noon, the regiment not even a regiment yet but merely a voluntary association of untried men who knew they were ignorant and hoped they were brave, the four sides of the Square lined with their fathers or grandfathers and their mothers and wives and sisters and sweethearts, the only uniform

present yet that one in which Sartoris stood with his
virgin sabre and his pristine colonel's braid on the courthouse balcony, bareheaded too while the Baptist minister
prayed and the Richmond mustering officer swore the
regiment in; and then (the regiment) gone; and now not
only the jail but the town too hung without motion
in a tideless backwash: the plunging body advanced far
enough now into space as to have lost all sense of motion,
weightless and immobile upon the light pressure of invisible air, gone now all diminishment of the precipice's
lip, all increment of the vast increaseless earth: a town of
old men and women and children and an occasional
wounded soldier (John Sartoris himself, deposed from his
colonelcy by a regimental election after Second Manassas,
came home and oversaw the making and harvesting of a
crop on his plantation before he got bored and gathered
up a small gang of irregular cavalry and carried it up into
Tennessee to join Forrest), static *in quo*, rumoured, mur-
mured of war only as from a great and incredible dreamy
distance, like far summer thunder: until the spring of '64,
the once-vast fixed impalpable increaseless and threatless
earth now one omnivorous roar of rock (a roar so vast
and so spewing, flinging ahead of itself, like the spray
above the maelstrom, the preliminary anæsthetic of shock
so that the agony of bone and flesh will not even be felt,
as to contain and sweep along with it the beginning, the
first ephemeral phase, of this story, permitting it to boil
for an instant to the surface like a chip or a twig—a
match-stick or a bubble, say, too weightless to give
resistance for destruction to function against: in this case,
a bubble, a minute globule which was its own impunity,
since what it—the bubble—contained, having no part in

rationality and being contemptuous of fact, was immune
even to the rationality of rock)—a sudden battle centring
around Colonel Sartoris's plantation house four miles to
the north, the line of a creek held long enough for the
main Confederate body to pass through Jefferson to a
stronger line on the river heights south of the town, a
rear-guard action of cavalry in the streets of the town
itself (and this was the story, the beginning of it; all of it
too, the town might have been justified in thinking, pre-
suming they had had time to see, notice, remark and then
remember, even that little)—the rattle and burst of pistols,
the hooves, the dust, the rush and scurry of a handful of
horsemen led by a lieutenant, up the street past the jail,
and the two of them—the frail and useless girl musing in
the blonde mist of her hair beside the window-pane where
three or four (or whatever it was) years ago she had
inscribed with her grandmother's diamond ring her para-
doxical and significantless name (and where, so it seemed
to the town, she had been standing ever since), and the
soldier, gaunt and tattered, battle-grimed and fleeing and
undefeated, looking at one another for that moment
across the fury and pell-mell of battle;

Then gone; that night the town was occupied by Federal
troops; two nights later, it was on fire (the Square, the
stores and shops and the professional offices), gutted (the
courthouse too), the blackened jagged topless jumbles
of brick wall enclosing like a ruined jaw the blackened
shell of the courthouse between its two rows of topless
columns, which (the columns) were only blackened and
stained, being tougher than fire: but not the jail, it
escaped, untouched, insulated by its windless backwater

from fire; and now the town was as though insulated by
fire or perhaps cauterised by fire from fury and turmoil,
the long roar of the rushing omnivorous rock fading on
to the east with the fading uproar of the battle: and so in
effect it was a whole year in advance of Appomattox (only
the undefeated undefeatable women, vulnerable only to
death, resisted, endured, irreconcilable); already, before
there was a name for them (already their prototype before
they even existed as a species), there were carpetbaggers
in Jefferson—a Missourian named Redmond, a cotton-
and quartermaster-supplies speculator, who had followed
the Northern army to Memphis in '61 and (nobody knew
exactly how or why) had been with (or at least on the
fringe of) the military household of the brigadier commanding the force which occupied Jefferson, himself—
Redmond—going no farther, stopping, staying, none
knew the why for that either, why he elected Jefferson,
chose that alien fire-gutted site (himself one, or at least
the associate, of them who had set the match) to be his
future home; and a German private, a blacksmith, a
deserter from a Pennsylvania regiment, who appeared in
the summer of '64, riding a mule, with (so the tale told
later, when his family of daughters had become matri-
archs and grandmothers of the town's new aristocracy)
for saddle-blanket sheaf on sheaf of virgin and uncut
United States banknotes, so Jefferson and Yoknapatawpha
County had mounted Golgotha and passed beyond
Appomattox a full year in advance, with returned soldiers
in the town, not only the wounded from the battle of
Jefferson, but whole men: not only the furloughed from
Forrest in Alabama and Johnston in Georgia and Lee in
Virginia, but the stragglers, the unmaimed flotsam and

refuse of that single battle now drawing its final constrict-
ing loop from the Atlantic Ocean at Old Point Comfort,
to Richmond: to Chattanooga: to Atlanta: to the Atlantic
Ocean again at Charleston, who were not deserters but
who could not rejoin any still-intact Confederate unit for
the reason that there were enemy armies between, so that
in the almost faded twilight of that land, the knell of
Appomattox made no sound; when in the spring and
early summer of '65 the formally and officially paroled
and disbanded soldiers began to trickle back into the
county, there was anticlimax; they returned to a land
which not only had passed through Appomattox over a
year ago, it had had that year in which to assimilate it,
that whole year in which not only to ingest surrender but
(begging the metaphor, the figure) to convert, meta-
bolise it, and then defæcate it as fertiliser for the four-
years' fallow land they were already in train to rehabili-
tate a year before the Virginia knell rang the formal
change, the men of '65 returning to find themselves alien
in the very land they had been bred and born in and had
fought for four years to defend, to find a working and
already solvent economy based on the premise that it
could get along without them; (and now the rest of this
story, since it occurs, happens, here: not yet June in '65;
this one had indeed wasted no time getting back: a
stranger, alone; the town did not even know it had ever
seen him before, because the other time was a year ago
and had lasted only while he galloped through it firing
a pistol backward at a Yankee army, and he had been
riding a horse—a fine though a little too small and too
delicate blooded mare—where now he rode a big mule,
which for that reason—its size—was a better mule than the

horse was a horse, but it was still a mule, and of course
the town could not know that he had swapped the mare
for the mule on the same day that he traded his lieutenant's sabre—he still had the pistol—for the stocking
full of seed corn he had seen growing in a Pennsylvania
field and had not let even the mule have one mouthful of
it during the long journey across the ruined land between
the Atlantic seaboard and the Jefferson jail, riding up to
the jail at last, still gaunt and tattered and dirty and still
undefeated and not fleeing now but instead making or at
least planning a single-handed assault against what any
rational man would have considered insurmountable odds
[but then, that bubble had ever been immune to the
ephemeræ of facts]; perhaps, probably—without doubt:
apparently she had been standing leaning musing in it for
three or four years in 1864; nothing had happened since,
not in a land which had even anticipated Appomattox,
capable of shaking a meditation that rooted, that durable,
that veteran—the girl watched him get down and tie the
mule to the fence, and perhaps while he walked from the
fence to the door he even looked for a moment at her,
though possibly, perhaps even probably, not, since she
was not his immediate object now, he was not really concerned with her at the moment, because he had so little
time, he had none, really: still to reach Alabama and the
small hill farm which had been his father's and would not
be his, if—no, when—he could get there, and it had not
been ruined by four years of war and neglect, and even if
the land was still plantable, even if he could start planting
the stocking of corn tomorrow, he would be weeks and
even months late; during that walk to the door and as he
lifted his hand to knock on it, he must have thought with

a kind of weary and indomitable outrage of how, already
months late, he must still waste a day or maybe even two
or three of them before he could load the girl onto the
mule behind him and head at last for Alabama—this, at
a time when of all things he would require patience and
a clear head, trying for them [courtesy too, which would
be demanded now], patient and urgent and polite, undefeated, trying to explain, in terms which they could
understand or at least accept, his simple need and the
urgency of it, to the mother and father whom he had
never seen before and whom he never intended, or anyway anticipated, to see again, not that he had anything
for or against them either: he simply intended to be too
busy for the rest of his life, once they could get on the
mule and start for home; not seeing the girl then, during
the interview, not even asking to see her for a moment
when the interview was over, because he had to get the
licence now and then find the preacher: so that the first
word he ever spoke to her was a promise delivered
through a stranger; it was probably not until they were
on the mule—the frail useless hands whose only strength
seemed to be that sufficient to fold the wedding licence
into the bosom of her dress and then cling to the belt
around his waist—that he looked at her again or [both of
them] had time to learn one another's middle name);

That was the story, the incident, ephemeral of an afternoon in late May, unrecorded by the town and the county
because they had little time too: which (the county and
the town) had anticipated Appomattox and kept that
lead, so that in effect Appomattox itself never overhauled
them; it was the long pull of course, but they had—as

they would realise later—that priceless, that unmatchable
year; on New Year's Day, 1865, while the rest of the
South sat staring at the north-east horizon beyond which
Richmond lay, like a family staring at the closed door to
a sick-room, Yoknapatawpha County was already nine
months gone in reconstruction; by New Year's of '66, the
gutted walls (the rain of two winters had washed them
clean of the smoke and soot) of the Square had been tem-
porarily roofed and were stores and shops and offices
again, and they had begun to restore the courthouse: not
temporary, this, but restored, exactly as it had been,
between the too columned porticoes, one north and one
south, which had been tougher than dynamite and fire,
because it was the symbol: the County and the City: and
they knew how, who had done it before; Colonel Sartoris
was home now, and General Compson, the first Jason
son, and though a tragedy had happened to Sutpen and
his pride—a failure not of his pride nor even of his own
bones and flesh, but of the lesser bones and flesh which
he had believed capable of supporting the edifice of his
dream—they still had the old plans of his architect and
even the architect's moulds, and even more: money,
(strangely, curiously) Redmond, the town's domesticated
carpetbagger, symbol of a blind rapacity almost like
a biological instinct, destined to cover the South like a
migration of locusts; in the case of this man, arriving
a full year before its time and now devoting no small
portion of the fruit of his rapacity to restoring the very
building the destruction of which had rung up the
curtain for his appearance on the stage, had been the
formal visa on his passport to pillage; and by New Year's
of '76, this same Redmond with his money and Colonel

Sartoris and General Compson had built a railroad from
Jefferson north into Tennessee to connect with the one
from Memphis to the Atlantic Ocean; nor content there
either, north or south: another ten years (Sartoris and
Redmond and Compson quarrelled, and Sartoris and
Redmond bought—probably with Redmond's money—
Compson's interest in the railroad, and the next year
Sartoris and Redmond had quarrelled and the year after
that, because of simple physical fear, Redmond killed
Sartoris from ambush on the Jefferson Square and fled,
and at last even Sartoris's supporters—he had no friends:
only enemies and frantic admirers—began to understand
the result of that regimental election in the fall of '62)
and the railroad was a part of that system covering the
whole South and East like the veins in an oak leaf and
itself mutually adjunctive to the other intricate systems
covering the rest of the United States, so that you could
get on a train in Jefferson now and, by changing and
waiting a few times, go anywhere in North America;

No more into the United States, but into the *rest* of the
United States, because the long pull was over now; only
the ageing unvanquished women were unreconciled, irreconcilable, reversed and irrevocably reverted against the
whole moving unanimity of panorama until, old un-
ordered vacant pilings above a tide's flood, they themselves had an illusion of motion, facing irreconcilably
backward toward the old lost battles, the old aborted
cause, the old four ruined years whose very physical
scars ten and twenty and twenty-five changes of season
had annealed back into the earth; twenty-five and then
thirty-five years; not only a century and an age, but a

way of thinking died; the town itself wrote the epilogue
and epitaph: 1900, on Confederate Decoration Day,
Mrs. Virginia Depre, Colonel Sartoris's sister, twitched
a lanyard and the spring-restive bunting collapsed and
flowed, leaving the marble effigy—the stone infantryman
on his stone pedestal on the exact spot where forty years
ago the Richmond officer and the local Baptist minister
had mustered in the Colonel's regiment, and the old men
in the grey and braided coats (all officers now, none less
in rank than captain) tottered into the sunlight and fired
shotguns at the bland sky and raised their cracked quaver-
ing voices in the shrill hackle-lifting yelling which Lee
and Jackson and Longstreet and the two Johnstons (and
Grant and Sherman and Hooker and Pope and McClellan
and Burnside too for the matter of that) had listened to
amid the smoke and the din; epilogue and epitaph, because apparently neither the U.D.C. ladies who instigated
and bought the monument, nor the architect who
designed it nor the masons who erected it, had noticed
that the marble eyes under the shading marble palm
stared not toward the north and the enemy, but toward
the south, toward (if anything) his own rear—looking
perhaps, the wits said (could say now, with the old war
thirty-five years past and you could even joke about it—
except the women, the ladies, the unsurrendered, the irreconcilable, who even after another thirty-five years would
still get up and stalk out of picture houses showing *Gone
With the Wind*), for reinforcements; or perhaps not a
combat soldier at all, but a provost marshal's man looking
for deserters, or perhaps himself for a safe place to run to:
because that old war was dead; the sons of those tottering
old men in grey had already died in blue coats in Cuba,

the macabre mementoes and testimonials and shrines of
the new war already usurping the earth before the blasts
of blank shotgun shells and the weightless collapsing of
bunting had unveiled the final ones to the old;

Not only a new century and a new way of thinking, but
of acting and behaving too: now you could go to bed in
a train in Jefferson and wake up tomorrow morning in
New Orleans or Chicago; there were electric lights and
running water in almost every house in town except the
cabins of Negroes; and now the town bought and brought
from a great distance a kind of grey crushed ballast-
stone called macadam, and paved the entire street between the depot and the hotel, so that no more would the
train-meeting hacks filled with drummers and lawyers
and court-witnesses need to lurch and heave and strain
through the winter mud-holes; every morning a wagon
came to your very door with artificial ice and put it in
your icebox on the back gallery for you, the children
in rotational neighbourhood gangs following it (the
wagon), eating the fragments of ice which the Negro
driver chipped off for them; and that summer a specially-
built sprinkling-cart began to make the round of the
streets each day; a new time, a new age: there were
screens in windows now; people (white people) could
actually sleep in summer night air, finding it harmless,
uninimical: as though there had waked suddenly in man
(or anyway in his womenfolks) a belief in his inalienable
civil right to be free of dust and bugs;

Moving faster and faster: from the speed of two horses
on either side of a polished tongue, to that of thirty then

fifty then a hundred under a tin bonnet no bigger than
a wash-tub: which from almost the first explosion,
would have to be controlled by police; already in a back
yard on the edge of town, an ex-blacksmith's-apprentice,
a grease-covered man with the eyes of a visionary monk,
was building a gasolene buggy, casting and boring his
own cylinders and rods and cams, inventing his own coils
and plugs and valves as he found he needed them, which
would run, and did: crept popping and stinking out of
the alley at the exact moment when the banker Bayard
Sartoris, the Colonel's son, passed in his carriage: as a
result of which, there is on the books of Jefferson today a
law prohibiting the operation of any mechanically-pro-
pelled vehicle on the streets of the corporate town: who
(the same banker Sartoris) died in one (such was progress,
that fast, that rapid) lost from control on an icy road by
his (the banker's) grandson, who had just returned from
(such was progress) two years of service as a combat air-
man on the Western Front and now the camouflage paint
is weathering slowly from a French ·75 field piece squatting on one flank of the base of the Confederate monument, but even before it faded there was neon in the town
and A.A.A. and C.C.C. in the county, and W.P.A. ('and
XYZ and etc.,' as 'Uncle Pete' Gombault, a lean clean
tobacco-chewing old man, incumbent of a political sinecure under the designation of United States marshal—an
office held back in reconstruction times, when the State
of Mississippi was a United States military district, by a
Negro man who was still living in 1925—fire-maker,
sweeper, janitor and furnace-attendant to five or six
lawyers and doctors and one of the banks—and still
known as 'Mulberry' from the avocation which he had

followed before and during and after his incumbency as
marshal: peddling illicit whiskey in pint and half-pint
bottles from a cache beneath the roots of a big mulberry
tree behind the drugstore of his pre-1865 owner—put it)
in both; W.P.A. and XYZ marking the town and the
county as war itself had not: gone now were the last of
the forest trees which had followed the shape of the
Square, shading the unbroken second-storey balcony
onto which the lawyers' and doctors' offices had opened,
which shaded in its turn the fronts of the stores and the
walkway beneath; and now was gone even the balcony
itself with its wrought-iron balustrade on which in the
long summer afternoons the lawyers would prop their
feet to talk; and the continuous iron chain looping from
wooden post to post along the circumference of the courthouse yard, for the farmers to hitch their teams to; and
the public watering trough where they could water them,
because gone was the last wagon to stand on the Square
during the spring and summer and fall Saturdays and
trading-days, and not only the Square but the streets
leading into it were paved now, with fixed signs of inter-
diction and admonition applicable only to something
capable of moving faster than thirty miles an hour; and
now the last forest tree was gone from the courthouse
yard too, replaced by formal synthetic shrubs contrived
and schooled in Wisconsin greenhouses, and in the courthouse (the city hall too) a courthouse and city hall gang,
in miniature of course (but that was not its fault but the
fault of the city's and the county's size and population
and wealth) but based on the pattern of Chicago and
Kansas City and Boston and Philadelphia (and which,
except for its minuscularity, neither Philadelphia nor

Boston nor Kansas City nor Chicago need have blushed
at) which every three or four years would try again to
raze the old courthouse in order to build a new one, not
that they did not like the old one nor wanted the new,
but because the new one would bring into the town and
county that much more increment of unearned federal
money;

And now the paint is preparing to weather from an anti-
tank howitzer squatting on rubber tyres on the opposite
flank of the Confederate monument; and gone now from
the fronts of the stores are the old bricks made of native
clay in Sutpen's architect's old moulds, replaced now by
sheets of glass taller than a man and longer than a wagon
and team, pressed intact in Pittsburgh factories and
framing interiors bathed now in one shadowless corpse-
glare of fluorescent light; and, now and at last, the last of
silence too: the county's hollow inverted air one resonant
boom and ululance of radio: and thus no more Yoknapatawpha's air nor even Mason and Dixon's air, but
America's: the patter of comedians, the baritone screams
of female vocalists, the babbling pressure to buy and buy
and still buy arriving more instantaneous than light, two
thousand miles from New York and Los Angeles; one
air, one nation: the shadowless fluorescent corpse-glare
bathing the sons and daughters of men and women,
Negro and white both, who were born to and who
passed all their lives in denim overalls and calico, haggling
by cash or the instalment-plan for garments copied last
week out of *Harper's Bazaar* or *Esquire* in East Side
sweat-shops: because an entire generation of farmers has
vanished, not just from Yoknapatawpha's but from

Mason and Dixon's earth: the self-consumer: the machine which displaced the man because the exodus of the man left no one to drive the mule, now that the machine was threatening to extinguish the mule; time was when the mules stood in droves at daylight in the plantation mule-lots across the plantation road from the serried identical ranks of two-room shotgun shacks in which lived in droves with his family the Negro tenant- or share- or furnish-hand who bridled him (the mule) in the lot at sun-up and followed him through the plumb-straight monotony of identical furrows and back to the lot at sun-down, with (the man) one eye on where the mule was going and the other eye on his (the mule's) heels; both gone now: the one, to the last of the forty- and fifty- and sixty-acre hill farms inaccessible from unmarked dirt roads, the other to New York and Detroit and Chicago and Los Angeles ghettos, or nine out of ten of him that is, the tenth one mounting from the handles of a plough to the springless bucket seat of a tractor, dispossessing and displacing the other nine just as the tractor had dispossessed and displaced the other eighteen mules to whom that nine would have been complement; then Warsaw and Dunkerque displaced that tenth in his turn, and now the planter's not-yet-drafted son drove the tractor: and then Pearl Harbour and Tobruk and Utah Beach displaced that son, leaving the planter himself on the seat of the tractor, for a little while that is—or so he thought, forgetting that victory or defeat both are bought at the same exorbitant price of change and alteration; one nation, one world: young men who had never been farther from Yoknapatawpha County than Memphis or New Orleans (and that not often), now talked glibly of street intersections in Asiatic and European capitals, returning no more to inherit the long monotonous endless unendable furrows of Mississippi cotton fields, living now (with now a wife and next year a wife and child and the year after that a wife and children) in automobile trailers or G.I. barracks on the outskirts of liberal arts colleges, and the father and now grandfather himself still driving the tractor across the gradually diminishing fields between the long looping skeins of electric lines bringing electric power from the Appalachian mountains, and the subterranean steel veins bringing the natural gas from the Western plains, to the little lost lonely farmhouses glittering and gleaming with automatic stoves and washing machines and television antennæ;

One nation: no longer anywhere, not even in Yoknapatawpha County, one last irreconcilable fastness of stronghold from which to enter the United States, because at last even the last old sapless indomitable unvanquished widow or maiden aunt had died and the old deathless Lost Cause had become a faded (though still select) social club or caste, or form of behaviour when you remembered to observe it on the occasions when young men from Brooklyn, exchange students at Mississippi or Arkansas or Texas Universities, vended tiny Confederate battle flags among the thronged Saturday afternoon ramps of football stadia; one world: the tank gun: captured from a regiment of Germans in an African desert by a regiment of Japanese in American uniforms, whose mothers and fathers at the time were in a California detention camp for enemy aliens, and carried (the gun) seven thousand miles back to be set halfway between, as

a sort of secondary flying buttress to a memento of
Shiloh and The Wilderness; one universe, one cosmos:
contained in one America: one towering frantic edifice
poised like a card-house over the abyss of the mortgaged
generations; one boom, one peace: one swirling rocket-
roar filling the glittering zenith as with golden feathers,
until the vast hollow sphere of his air, the vast and
terrible burden beneath which he tries to stand erect and
lift his battered and indomitable head—the very substance in which he lives and, lacking which, he would
vanish in a matter of seconds—is murmurous with his
fears and terrors and disclaimers and repudiations and his
aspirations and dreams and his baseless hopes, bouncing
back at him in radar waves from the constellations;

And still—the old jail—endured, sitting in its rumourless
cul-de-sac, its almost seasonless backwater in the middle
of that rush and roar of civic progress and social alteration and change like a collarless (and reasonably clean:
merely dingy: with a day's stubble and no garters to his
socks) old man sitting in his suspenders and stocking feet,
on the back kitchen steps inside a walled courtyard;
actually not isolated by location so much as insulated by
obsolescence: on the way out of course (to disappear from
the surface of the earth along with the rest of the town
on the day when all America, after cutting down all the
trees and levelling the hills and mountains with bull-
dozers, would have to move underground to make room
for, get out of the way of, the motor-cars) but like the
track-walker in the tunnel, the thunder of the express
mounting behind him, who finds himself opposite a niche
or crack exactly his size in the wall's living and impreg-

nable rock, and steps into it, inviolable and secure while destruction roars past and on and away, grooved ineluctably to the spidery rails of its destiny and destination; not even—the jail—worth selling to the United States for some matching allocation out of the federal treasury; not even (so fast, so far, was Progress) any more a real pawn, let alone knight or rook, on the County's political board, not even plum in true worth of the word: simply a modest sinecure for the husband of someone's cousin, who had failed not as a father but merely as a fourth-rate farmer or day-labourer;

It survived, endured; it had its inevictable place in the town and the county; it was even still adding modestly not just to its but to the town's and the county's history too: somewhere behind that dingy brick façade, between the old durable hand-moulded brick and the cracked creosote-impregnated plaster of the inside walls (though few in the town or county any longer knew that they were there) were the old notched and morticed logs which (this, the town and county did remember; it was part of its legend) had held someone who might have been Wiley Harpe; during that summer of 1864, the federal brigadier who had fired the Square and the courthouse had used the jail as his provost-marshal's guard-house; and even children in high school remembered how the jail had been host to the Governor of the State while he discharged a thirty-day sentence for contempt of court for refusing to testify in a paternity suit brought against one of his lieutenants: but isolate, even its legend and record and history, indisputable in authenticity yet a little oblique, elliptic or perhaps just ellipsoid, washed thinly over with a faint quiet cast of apocrypha: because there were new people in the town now, strangers, outlanders, living in new minute glass-walled houses set as neat and orderly and antiseptic as cribs in a nursery ward, in new sub-divisions named Fairfield or Longwood or Halcyon Acres which had once been the lawn or back yard or kitchen garden of the old residences (the old obsolete columned houses still standing among them like old horses surged suddenly out of slumber in the middle of a flock of sheep), who had never seen the jail; that is, they had looked at it in passing, they knew where it was, when their kin or friends or acquaintances from the East or North or California visited them or passed through Jefferson on the way to New Orleans or Florida, they could even repeat some of its legend or history to them: but they had had no contact with it; it was not a part of their lives; they had the automatic stoves and furnaces and milk deliveries and lawns the size of instalment-plan rugs; they had never had to go to the jail on the morning after June Tenth or July Fourth or Thanksgiving or Christmas or New Year's (or for that matter, on almost any Monday morning) to pay the fine of house-man or gardener or handyman so that he could hurry on home (still wearing his hangover or his barely-staunched razor-slashes) and milk the cow or clean the furnace or mow the lawn;

So only the old citizens knew the jail any more, not old people but old citizens: men and women old not in years but in the constancy of the town, or against that con-stancy, concordant (not coeval of course, the town's date was a century and a quarter ago now, but in accord against that continuation) with that thin durable con-

tinuity born a hundred and twenty-five years ago out of
a handful of bandits captured by a drunken militia squad,
and a bitter ironical incorruptible wilderness mail-rider,
and a monster wrought-iron padlock—that steadfast and
durable and unhurryable continuity against or across
which the vain and glittering ephemeræ of progress and
alteration washed in substanceless repetitive evanescent
scarless waves, like the wash and glare of the neon sign on
what was still known as the Holston House diagonally
opposite, which would fade with each dawn from the
old brick walls of the jail and leave no trace; only the old
citizens still knew it: the intractable and obsolescent of the
town who still insisted on wood-burning ranges and cows
and vegetable gardens and handymen who had to be
taken out of hock on the mornings after Saturday nights
and holidays; or the ones who actually spent the Saturday-
and holiday-nights inside the barred doors and windows
of the cells or bullpen for drunkenness or fighting or
gambling—the servants, housemen and gardeners and
handymen, who would be extracted the next morning by
their white folks, and the others (what the town knew as
the New Negro, independent of that commodity) who
would sleep there every night beneath the thin ruby
chequer-barred wash and fade of the hotel sign, while
they worked their fines out on the street; and the County,
since its cattle-thieves and moonshiners went to trial from
there, and its murderers—by electricity now (so fast, that
fast, was Progress)—to eternity from there; in fact it was
still, not a factor perhaps, but at least an integer, a cipher,
in the county's political establishment; at least still used
by the Board of Supervisors, if not as a lever, at least
as something like Punch's stuffed club, not intended

to break bones, not aimed to leave any permanent scars;

So only the old knew it, the irreconcilable Jeffersonians and Yoknapatawphians who had (and without doubt firmly intended to continue to have) actual personal dealings with it on the blue Monday mornings after holidays, or during the semi-yearly terms of Circuit or Federal Court:—until suddenly you, a stranger, an outlander say from the East or the North or the Far West, passing through the little town by simple accident, or perhaps relation or acquaintance or friend of one of the outland families which had moved into one of the pristine and recent subdivisions, yourself turning out of your way to fumble among road signs and filling stations out of frank curiosity, to try to learn, comprehend, understand what had brought your cousin or friend or acquaintance to elect to live here—not specifically here, of course, not specifically Jefferson, but such as here, such as Jefferson—suddenly you would realise that something curious was happening or had happened here: that instead of dying off as they should as time passed it was as though these old irreconcilables were actually increasing in number; as though with each interment of one, two more shared that vacancy: where in 1900, only thirty-five years afterward, there could not have been more than two or three capable of it, either by knowledge or memory of leisure, or even simple willingness and inclination, now, in 1951, eighty-six years afterward, they could be counted in dozens (and in 1965, a hundred years afterward, in hundreds because —by now you had already begun to understand why your kin or friends or acquaintance had elected to come

to such as this with his family and call it his life—by then
the children of that second outland invasion following a
war, would also have become not just Mississippians but
Jeffersonians and Yoknapatawphians: by which time—
who knows?—not merely the pane, but the whole window, perhaps the entire wall, may have been removed
and embalmed intact into a museum by an historical, or
anyway a cultural, club of ladies—why, by that time
they may not even know, or even need to know: only
that the window-pane bearing the girl's name and the
date is that old, which is enough; has lasted that long: one
small rectangle of wavy, crudely-pressed, almost opaque
glass, bearing a few faint scratches apparently no more
durable than the thin dried slime left by the passage of a
snail, yet which has endured a hundred years) who are
capable and willing too to quit whatever they happen to
be doing—sitting on the last of the wooden benches
beneath the last of the locust and chinaberry trees among
the potted conifers of the new age dotting the courthouse
yard, or in the chairs along the shady sidewalk before the
Holston House, where a breeze always blows—to lead
you across the street and into the jail and (with courteous
neighbourly apologies to the jailor's wife stirring or turning on the stove the peas and grits and side-meat—pur-
chased in bargain-lot quantities by shrewd and inde-
fatigable peditation from store to store—which she will
serve to the prisoners for dinner or supper at so much a
head—plate—payable by the County, which is no mean
factor in the sinecure of her husband's incumbency) into
the kitchen and so to the cloudy pane bearing the faint
scratches which, after a moment, you will descry to be
a name and a date;

Not at first, of course, but after a moment, a second, because at first you would be a little puzzled, a little impatient because of your illness-at-ease from having been dragged without warning or preparation into the private kitchen of a strange woman cooking a meal; you would think merely *What? So what?* annoyed and even a little outraged, until suddenly, even while you were thinking it, something has already happened: the faint frail illegible meaningless even inference-less scratching on the ancient poor-quality glass you stare at, has moved, under your eyes, even while you stared at it, coalesced, seeming actually to have entered into another sense than vision: a scent, a whisper, filling that hot cramped strange room already fierce with the sound and reek of frying pork-fat: the two of them in conjunction—the old milky obsolete glass, and the scratches on it: that tender ownerless obsolete girl's name and the old dead date in April almost a century ago—speaking, murmuring, back from, out of, across from, a time as old as lavender, older than album or stereopticon, as old as daguerreo-type itself;

And being a stranger and a guest would have been enough, since, a stranger and a guest, you would have shown the simple courtesy and politeness of asking the questions naturally expected of you by the host or anyway volunteer guide, who had dropped whatever he was doing (even if that had been no more than sitting with others of his like on a bench in a courthouse yard or on the sidewalk before a hotel) in order to bring you here; not to mention your own perfectly natural desire for, not revenge perhaps, but at least compensation, restitution, vindication, for the shock and annoyance of having been

brought here without warning or preparation, into the
private quarters of a strange woman engaged in something as intimate as cooking a meal; but by now you had
not only already begun to understand why your kin or
friend or acquaintance had elected, not Jefferson but such
as Jefferson, for his life, but you had heard that voice, that
whisper, murmur, frailer than the scent of lavender, yet
(for that second anyway) louder than all the seethe and
fury of frying fat; so you ask the questions, not only
which are expected of you, but whose answers you yourself must have if you are to get back into your car and
fumble with any attention and concentration among the
road signs and filling stations, to get on to wherever it is
you had started when you stopped by chance or accident
in Jefferson for an hour or a day or a night, and the host
—guide—answers them, to the best of his ability out of
the town's composite heritage of remembering that long
back, told, repeated, bequeathed to him by his father; or
rather, his mother: from her mother: or better still, to
him when he himself was a child, direct from his great-
aunt: the spinsters, maiden and childless out of a time
when there were too many women because too many of
the young men were maimed or dead: the indomitable
and undefeated, maiden progenitresses of spinster and
childless descendants still capable of rising up and stalking
out in the middle of *Gone With the Wind*;

And again one sense assumes the office of two or three:
not only hearing, listening, and seeing too, but you are
even standing on the same spot, the same boards she did
that day she wrote her name into the window and on the
other one three years later watching and hearing through

and beyond that faint fragile defacement the sudden rush
and thunder: the dust: the crackle and splatter of pistols:
then the face, gaunt, battle-dirty, stubbled-over; urgent
of course, but merely harried, harassed; not defeated,
turned for a fleeing instant across the turmoil and the
fury, then gone: and still the girl in the window (the
guide—host—has never said one or the other; without
doubt in the town's remembering after a hundred years
it has changed that many times from blonde to dark and
back to blonde again: which doesn't matter, since in your
own remembering that tender mist and veil will be forever blonde) not even waiting: musing; a year, and still
not even waiting: meditant, not even unimpatient: just
patienceless, in the sense that blindness and zenith are
colourless; until at last the mule, not out of the long
north-eastern panorama of defeat and dust and fading
smoke, but drawn out of it by that impregnable, that invincible, that incredible, that terrifying passivity, coming
at that one fatigueless unflagging job all the way from
Virginia—the mule which was a better mule in 1865 than
the blood mare had been a horse in '-2 and '-3 and '-4,
for the reason that this was now 1865, and the man, still
gaunt and undefeated: merely harried and urgent and
short of time to get on to Alabama and see the condition
of his farm—or (for that matter) if he still had a farm,
and now the girl, the fragile and workless girl not only
incapable of milking a cow but of whom it was never
even demanded required, suggested, that she substitute
for her father in drying the dishes, mounting pillion on
a mule behind a paroled cavalry subaltern out of a surrendered army who had swapped his charger for a mule
and the sabre of his rank and his defeatless pride for a

stocking full of seed corn, whom she had not known or
even spoken to long enough to have learned his middle
name or his preference in food, or told him hers, and
no time for that even now: riding, hurrying toward a
country she had never seen, to begin a life which was
not even simple frontier, engaged only with wilderness
and shoeless savages and the tender hand of God but one
which had been rendered into a desert (assuming that it
was still there at all to be returned to) by the iron and
fire of civilisation;

Which was all your host (guide) could tell you, since that
was all he knew, inherited, inheritable from the town:
which was enough, more than enough in fact, since all
you needed was the face framed in its blonde and delicate
veil behind the scratched glass; yourself, the stranger, the
outlander from New England or the prairies or the
Pacific Coast, no longer come by the chance or accident
of kin or friend or acquaintance or road map, but drawn
too from ninety years away by that incredible and terrifying passivity, watching in your turn through and beyond
that old milk-dim disfigured glass that shape, that delicate
frail and useless bone and flesh departing pillion on a mule
without one backward look, to the reclaiming of an
abandoned and doubtless even ravaged (perhaps even
usurped) Alabama hill farm—being lifted on to the mule
(the first time he touched her probably, except to put the
ring on: not to prove nor even to feel, touch, if there
actually was a girl under the calico and the shawls; there
was no time for that yet; but simply to get her up so
they could start), to ride a hundred miles to become the
farmless mother of farmers (she would bear a dozen, all

boys, herself no older, still fragile, still workless among
the churns and stove and brooms and stacks of wood
which even a woman could split into kindlings; unchanged), bequeathing to them in their matronymic the
heritage of that invincible inviolable ineptitude;

Then suddenly, you realise that that was nowhere near
enough, not for that face—bridehood, motherhood,
grandmotherhood, then widowhood and at last the grave
—the long peaceful connubial progress toward matriarchy in a rocking chair nobody else was allowed to sit
in, then a headstone in a country churchyard—not for
that passivity, that stasis, that invincible captaincy of soul
which didn't even need to wait but simply to be, breathe
tranquilly, and take food—infinite not only in capacity
but in scope too: that face, one maiden muse which had
drawn a man out of the running pell-mell of a cavalry
battle, a whole year around the long iron perimeter of
duty and oath, from Yoknapatawpha County, Mississippi, across Tennessee into Virginia and up to the fringe
of Pennsylvania before it curved back into its closing fade
along the headwaters of the Appomattox river and at last
removed from him its iron hand: where, a safe distance at
last into the rainy woods from the picket lines and the
furled flags and the stacked muskets, a handful of men
leading spent horses, the still-warm pistols still loose and
quick for the hand in the unstrapped scabbards, gathered
in the failing twilight—privates and captains, sergeants
and corporals and subalterns—talking a little of one last
desperate cast southward where (by last report) Johnston
was still intact, knowing that they would not, that they
were done not only with vain resistance but with in-

domitability too; already departed this morning in fact
for Texas, the West, New Mexico: a new land even if
not yet (spent too—like the horses—from the long
harassment and anguish of remaining indomitable and
undefeated) a new hope, putting behind them for good
and all the lost of both: the young dead bride—drawing
him (that face) even back from this too, from no longer
having to remain undefeated too: who swapped the
charger for the mule and the sabre for the stocking of
seed corn: back across the whole ruined land and the
whole disastrous year by that virgin inevictable passivity
more inescapable than lodestar;

Not that face; that was nowhere near enough: no symbol
there of connubial matriarchy, but fatal instead with all
insatiate and deathless sterility; spouseless, barren, and un-
descended; not even demanding more than that: simply
requiring it, requiring all—Lilith's lost and insatiable face
drawing the substance—the will and hope and dream and
imagination—of all men (you too: yourself and the host
too) into that one bright fragile net and snare; not even
to be caught, over-flung, by one single unerring cast of
it, but drawn to watch in patient and thronging turn the
very weaving of the strangling golden strands—drawing
the two of you from almost a hundred years away in your
turn—yourself the stranger, the outlander with a B.A. or
(perhaps even) M.A. from Harvard or Northwestern or
Stanford, passing through Jefferson by chance or accident
on the way to somewhere else, and the host who in three
generations has never been out of Yoknapatawpha
farther than a few prolonged Saturday nights in Memphis
or New Orleans, who has heard of Jenny Lind, not

because he has heard of Mark Twain and Mark Twain spoke well of her, but for the same reason that Mark Twain spoke well of her: not that she sang songs, but that she sang them in the old West in the old days, and the man sanctioned by public affirmation to wear a pistol openly in his belt is an inevictable part of the Missouri and the Yoknapatawpha dream too, but never of Duse or Bernhardt or Maximilian of Mexico, let alone whether the Emperor of Mexico even ever had a wife or not (saying—the host—: 'You mean, she was one of them? maybe even that emperor's wife?' and you: 'Why not? Wasn't she a Jefferson girl?')—to stand, in this hot strange little room furious with frying fat, among the roster and chronicle, the deathless murmur of the sublime and deathless names and the deathless faces, the faces omnivorous and insatiable and forever incontent: demon-nun and angel-witch; empress, siren, Erinys: Mistinguette, too, invincibly possessed of a half-century more of years than the mere threescore or so she bragged and boasted, for you to choose among, which one she was—not *might* have been, nor even *could* have been, but *was*: so vast, so limitless in capacity is man's imagination to disperse and burn away the rubble-dross of fact and probability, leaving only truth and dream—then gone, you are outside again, in the hot noon sun: late; you have already wasted too much time: to unfumble among the road signs and filling stations to get back on to a highway you know, back into the United States; not that it matters, since you know again now that there is no time: no space: no distance: a fragile and workless scratching almost depthless in a sheet of old barely transparent glass, and (all you had to do was look at it a while; all you have to do now is remember it) there is the clear undistanced voice as though out of the delicate antenna-skeins of radio, further than empress's throne, than splendid insatiation, even than matriarch's peaceful rocking chair, across the vast instantaneous intervention, from the long long time ago: '*Listen, stranger; this was myself: this was I.*'

Interior, the Jail. 10.30 A.M. March twelfth.

The common room, or 'bull-pen.' It is on the second floor. A heavy barred door at left is the entrance to it, to the entire cell-block, which—the cells—are indicated by a row of steel doors, each with its own individual small barred window, lining the right wall. A narrow passage at the far end of the right wall leads to more cells. A single big heavily barred window in the rear wall looks down into the street. It is mid-morning of a sunny day.

The door, left, opens with a heavy clashing of the steel lock, and swings back and outward. Temple enters, followed by Stevens and the Jailor. Temple has changed her dress, but wears the fur coat and the same hat. Stevens is dressed exactly as he was in Act II. The Jailor is a typical small-town turnkey, in shirt-sleeves and no necktie, carrying the heavy keys on a big iron ring against his leg as a farmer carries a lantern, say. He is drawing the door to behind him as he enters.

Temple stops just inside the room. Stevens perforce stops also. The Jailor closes the door and locks it on the inside with another clash and clang of steel, and turns.

JAILOR
Well, Lawyer, singing school will be over after tonight, huh?
(to Temple)
You been away, you see. You don't know about this, you ain't up with what's——

(he stops himself quickly; he is about to commit what he would call a very bad impoliteness, what in the tenets of his class and kind would be the most grave of gaucherie and bad taste: referring directly to a recent bereavement in the presence of the bereaved, particularly one of this nature, even though by this time tomorrow the state itself will have made restitution with the perpetrator's life. He tries to rectify it)

Not that I wouldn't too, if I'd a been the ma of the very——

(stopping himself again; this is getting worse than ever; now he not only is looking at Stevens, but actually addressing him)

Every Sunday night, and every night since last Sunday except last night—come to think of it, Lawyer, where was you last night? We missed you—Lawyer here and Na—the prisoner have been singing hymns in her cell. The first time, he just stood out there on the sidewalk while she stood in that window yonder. Which was all right, not doing no harm, just singing church hymns. Because all of us home folks here in Jefferson and Yoknapatawpha County both know Lawyer Stevens, even if some of us might have thought he got a little out of line——

(again it is getting out of hand; he realises it, but there is nothing he can do now; he is like someone walking a foot-

H*

           log: all he can do is move as fast as he
           dares until he can reach solid ground or
           at least pass another log to leap to)
defending a nigger murderer let alone when it
was his own niece was mur——

           (and reaches another log and leaps to it
           without stopping: at least one running
           at right angles for a little distance into
           simple generality)

—maybe suppose some stranger say, some durn
Yankee tourist, happened to be passing through
in a car, when we get enough durn criticism from
Yankees like it is—besides, a white man standing
out there in the cold, while a durned nigger murderer is up here all warm and comfortable; so it
happened that me and Mrs. Tubbs hadn't went to
prayer meeting that night, so we invited him to
come in; and to tell the truth, we come to enjoy
it too. Because as soon as they found out there
wasn't going to be no objection to it, the other
nigger prisoners (I got five more right now, but
I taken them out back and locked them up in
the coal house so you could have some privacy)
joined in too, and by the second or third Sunday
night, folks was stopping along the street to listen
to them instead of going to regular church. Of
course, the other niggers would just be in and out
over Saturday and Sunday night for fighting or
gambling or vagrance or drunk, so just about the
time they would begin to get in tune, the whole
choir would be a complete turnover. In fact, I
had a idea at one time to have the Marshal comb

the nigger dives and joints not for drunks and
gamblers, but basses and baritones.

> (he starts to laugh, guffaws once, then
> catches himself; he looks at Temple with
> something almost gentle, almost articu-
> late, in his face, taking (as though) by
> the horns, facing frankly and openly the
> dilemma of his own inescapable vice)

Excuse me, Mrs. Stevens. I talk too much. All I
want to say is, this whole county, not a man or
woman, wife or mother either in the whole state
of Mississippi, that don't—don't feel——

> (stopping again, looking at Temple)

There I am, still at it, still talking too much.
Wouldn't you like for Mrs. Tubbs to bring you
up a cup of coffee or maybe a Coca-Cola? She's
usually got a bottle or two of sody pop in the
icebox.

TEMPLE
No, thank you, Mr. Tubbs. If we could just see
Nancy——

JAILOR
> (turning)

Sure, sure.

He crosses toward the rear, right, and disappears into
the passage.

TEMPLE
The blindfold again. Out of a Coca-Cola bottle
this time or a cup of county-owned coffee.

Stevens takes the same pack of cigarettes from his overcoat pocket, though Temple has declined before he can
even offer them.

No, thanks. My hide's toughened now. I hardly
feel it. People. They're really innately, inherently
gentle and compassionate and kind. That's what
wrings, wrenches . . . something. Your entrails,
maybe. The member of the mob who holds up
the whole ceremony for seconds or even minutes
while he dislodges a family of bugs or lizards from
the log he is about to put on the fire——

> (there is the clash of another steel door
> off-stage as the Jailor unlocks Nancy's
> cell. Temple pauses, turns and listens,
> then continues rapidly)

And now I've got to say 'I forgive you, sister'
to the nigger who murdered my baby. No: it's
worse: I've even got to transpose it, turn it around.
I've got to start off my new life being forgiven
again. How can I say that? Tell me. How can I?
She stops again and turns farther as Nancy enters from
the rear alcove, followed by the Jailor, who passes Nancy
and comes on, carrying the ring of keys once more like
a farmer's lantern.

JAILOR
> (to Stevens)

Okay, Lawyer. How much time you want?
Thirty minutes? an hour?

STEVENS
Ten minutes should be enough.

JAILOR
> (still moving toward the exit, left)

Okay.
> (to Temple)

You sure you don't want that coffee or a Coca-Cola? I could bring you up a rocking chair——

TEMPLE
Thank you just the same, Mr. Tubbs.

JAILOR
Okay.
(at the exit door, unlocking it)
Ten minutes, then.

He unlocks the door, opens it, exits, closes and locks it behind him; the lock clashes, his footsteps die away. Nancy has slowed and stopped where the Jailor passed her; she now stands about six feet to the rear of Temple and Stevens. Her face is calm, unchanged. She is dressed exactly as before, except for the apron; she still wears the hat.

NANCY
(to Temple)
You been to California, they tell me. I used to think maybe I would get there too, some day. But I waited too late to get around to it.

TEMPLE
So did I. Too late and too long. Too late when I went to California, and too late when I came back. That's it: too late and too long, not only for you, but for me too; already too late when both of us should have got around to running, like from death itself, from the very air anybody breathed named Drake or Mannigoe.

NANCY
Only, we didn't. And you come back, yesterday

evening. I heard that too. And I know where you
were last night, you and him both.
(indicating Stevens)
You went to see the Mayor.

TEMPLE

Oh, God, the mayor. No: the Governor, the Big
Man himself, in Jackson. Of course; you knew
that as soon as you realised that Mr. Gavin
wouldn't be here last night to help you sing,
didn't you? In fact, the only thing you can't know
about it is what the Governor told us. You can't
know that yet, no matter how clairvoyant you
are, because we—the Governor and Mr. Gavin
and I—were not even talking about you; the
reason I—we had to go and see him was not to
beg or plead or bind or loose, but because it would
be my right, my duty, my privilege—— Don't
look at me, Nancy.

NANCY

I'm not looking at you. Besides, it's all right. I
know what the Governor told you. Maybe I
could have told you last night what he would
say, and saved you the trip. Maybe I ought to
have—sent you the word as soon as I heard you
were back home, and knowed what you and
him——
(again she indicates Stevens with that
barely discernible movement of her
head, her hands still folded across her
middle as though she still wore the
absent apron)

—both would probably be up to. Only, I didn't.
But it's all right——

TEMPLE
Why didn't you? Yes, look at me. This is worse,
but the other is terrible.

NANCY
What?

TEMPLE
Why didn't you send me the word?

NANCY
Because that would have been hoping: the hardest
thing of all to break, get rid of, let go of, the last
thing of all poor sinning man will turn aloose.
Maybe it's because that's all he's got. Leastways,
he holds onto it, hangs onto it. Even with salvation
laying right in his hand, and all he's got to do is,
choose between it; even with salvation already in
his hand and all he needs is just to shut his fingers,
old sin is still too strong for him, and sometimes
before he even knows it, he has throwed salvation
away just grabbling back at hoping. But it's all
right——

STEVENS
You mean, when you have salvation, you don't
have hope?

NANCY
You don't even need it. All you need, all you have
to do, is just believe. So maybe——

STEVENS
Believe what?

NANCY

Just believe.—So maybe it's just as well that all I did last night, was just to guess where you all went. But I know now, and I know what the Big Man told you. And it's all right. I finished all that a long time back, that same day in the judge's court. No: before that even: in the nursery that night, before I even lifted my hand——

TEMPLE
(convulsively)
Hush. Hush.

NANCY

All right. I've hushed. Because it's all right. I can get low for Jesus too. I can get low for Him too.

TEMPLE

Hush! Hush! At least, don't blaspheme. But who am I to challenge the language you talk about Him in, when He Himself certainly can't challenge it, since that's the only language He arranged for you to learn?

NANCY

What's wrong with what I said? Jesus is a man too. He's got to be. Menfolks listens to somebody because of what he says. Women don't. They don't care what he said. They listens because of what he is.

TEMPLE

Then let Him talk to me. I can get low for Him too, if that's all He wants, demands, asks. I'll do anything He wants if He'll just tell me what to do.

No: how to do it. I know what to do, what I must
do, what I've got to do. But how? We—I thought
that all I would have to do would be to come back
and go to the Big Man and tell him that it wasn't
you who killed my baby, but I did it five years
ago that day when I slipped out the back door of
that train, and that would be all. But we were
wrong. Then I—we thought that all it would be
was, for me just to come back here and tell you
you had to die; to come all the way two thousand
miles from California, to sit up all night driving to
Jackson and talking for an hour or two and then
driving back, to tell you you had to die; not just
to bring you the news that you had to die, because
any messenger could do that, but just so it could
be me that would have to sit up all night and talk
for the hour or two hours and then bring you the
news back. You know: not to save you, that
wasn't really concerned in it: but just for me, just
for the suffering and the paying: a little more
suffering simply because there was a little more
time left for a little more of it, and we might as
well use it since we were already paying for it; and
that would be all; it would be finished then. But
we were wrong again. That was all, only for you.
You wouldn't be any worse off if I had never
come back from California. You wouldn't even
be any worse off. And this time tomorrow, you
won't be anything at all. But not me. Because
there's tomorrow, and tomorrow, and tomorrow.
All you've got to do is, just to die. But let Him
tell me what to do. No: that's wrong; I know

what to do, what I'm going to do; I found that
out that same night in the nursery too. But let
Him tell me how. How? Tomorrow, and tomorrow, and still tomorrow. How?

NANCY

Trust in Him.

TEMPLE

Trust in Him. Look what He has already done to
me. Which is all right; maybe I deserved it; at
least I'm not the one to criticise or dictate to Him.
But look what He did to you. Yet you can still
say that. Why? Why? Is it because there isn't anything else?

NANCY

I don't know. But you got to trust Him. Maybe
that's your pay for the suffering.

STEVENS

Whose suffering, and whose pay? Just each one's
for his own?

NANCY

Everybody's. All suffering. All poor sinning
man's.

STEVENS

The salvation of the world is in man's suffering.
Is that it?

NANCY

Yes, sir.

STEVENS

How?

NANCY

I don't know. Maybe when folks are suffering,
they will be too busy to get into devilment, won't
have time to worry and meddle one another.

TEMPLE

But why must it be suffering? He's omnipotent, or
so they tell us. Why couldn't He have invented
something else? Or, if it's got to be suffering, why
can't it be just your own? why can't you buy back
your own sins with your own agony? Why do you
and my little baby both have to suffer just because
I decided to go to a baseball game five years ago?
Do you have to suffer everybody else's anguish
just to believe in God? What kind of God is it that
has to blackmail His customers with the whole
world's grief and ruin?

NANCY

He don't want you to suffer.   He don't like suffering neither. But He can't help Himself. He's like
a man that's got too many mules. All of a sudden
one morning, he looks around and sees more mules
than he can count at one time even, let alone find
work for, and all he knows is that they are his,
because at least don't nobody else want to claim
them, and that the pasture fence was still holding
them last night where they can't harm themselves
nor nobody else the least possible. And that when
Monday morning comes, he can walk in there
and hem some of them up and even catch them if
he's careful about not never turning his back on
the ones he ain't hemmed up. And that, once the

gear is on them, they will do his work and do it good, only he's still got to be careful about getting too close to them, or forgetting that another one of them is behind him, even when he is feeding them. Even when it's Saturday noon again, and he is turning them back into the pasture, where even a mule can know it's got until Monday morning anyway to run free in mule sin and mule pleasure.

STEVENS
You have got to sin, too?

NANCY
You ain't *got* to. You can't help it. And He knows that. But you can suffer. And He knows that too. He don't tell you not to sin, he just asks you not to. And He don't tell you to suffer. But He gives you the chance. He gives you the best He can think of, that you are capable of doing. And He will save you.

STEVENS
You too? A murderess? In heaven?

NANCY
I can work.

STEVENS
The harp, the raiment, the singing, may not be for Nancy Mannigoe—not now. But there's still the work to be done—the washing and sweeping, maybe even the children to be tended and fed and kept from hurt and harm and out from under the grown folks' feet?

(he pauses a moment. Nancy says nothing, immobile, looking at no one)

Maybe even that baby?

(Nancy doesn't move, stir, not looking
at anything apparently, her face still, bemused, expressionless)

That one too, Nancy? Because you loved that
baby, even at the very moment when you raised
your hand against it, knew that there was nothing
left but to raise your hand?

(Nancy doesn't answer nor stir)

A heaven where that little child will remember
nothing of your hands but gentleness because now
this earth will have been nothing but a dream that
didn't matter? Is that it?

TEMPLE

Or maybe not that baby, not mine, because, since
I destroyed mine myself when I slipped out the
back end of that train that day five years ago, I
will need about all the forgiving and forgetting
that one six-months-old baby is capable of. But
the other one: yours: that you told me about, that
you were carrying six months gone, and you went
to the picnic or dance or frolic or fight or whatever it was, and the man kicked you in the stomach
and you lost it? That one too?

STEVENS

(to Nancy)

What? Its father kicked you in the stomach while
you were pregnant?

NANCY

I don't know.

STEVENS

You don't know who kicked you?

NANCY

I know that. I thought you meant its pa.

STEVENS

You mean, the man, who kicked you wasn't even
its father?

NANCY

I don't know. Any of them might have been.

STEVENS

Any of them? You don't have any idea who its
father was?

NANCY

(looks at Stevens impatiently)
If you backed your behind into a buzz-saw, could
you tell which tooth hit you first?
(to Temple)
What about that one?

TEMPLE

Will that one be there too, that never had a father
and never was even born, to forgive you? Is there
a heaven for it to go to so it can forgive you? Is
there a heaven, Nancy?

NANCY

I don't know. I believes.

TEMPLE
Believe what?

NANCY
I don't know. But I believes.

They all pause at the sound of feet approaching beyond
the exit door, all are looking at the door as the key
clashes again in the lock and the door swings out and the
Jailor enters, drawing the door to behind him.

JAILOR
(locking the door)
Thirty minutes, Lawyer. You named it, you
know: not me.

STEVENS
I'll come back later.

JAILOR
(turns and crosses toward them)
Provided you don't put it off too late. What I
mean, if you wait until tonight to come back,
you might have some company; and if you
put it off until tomorrow, you won't have no
client.
(to Nancy)
I found that preacher you want. He'll be here
about sundown, he said. He sounds like he might
even be another good baritone. And you can't
have too many, especially as after tonight you
won't need none, huh? No hard feelings, Nancy.
You committed about as horrible a crime as this
county ever seen, but you're fixing to pay the law
for it, and if the child's own mother——

> (he falters, almost pauses, catches him-
> self and continues briskly, moving
> again)

There, talking too much again. Come on, if
Lawyer's through with you. You can start taking
your time at daylight tomorrow morning, because you might have a long hard trip.

He passes her and goes briskly on toward the alcove at
rear. Nancy turns to follow.

TEMPLE
> (quickly)

Nancy.

> (Nancy doesn't pause. Temple continues,
> rapidly)

What about me? Even if there is one and somebody waiting in it to forgive me, there's still
tomorrow and tomorrow. And suppose tomorrow
and tomorrow, and then nobody there, nobody
waiting to forgive me——

NANCY
> (moving on after the Jailor)

Believe.

TEMPLE
Believe what, Nancy? Tell me.

NANCY
Believe.

She exits into the alcove behind the Jailor. The steel door
off-stage clangs, the key clashes. Then the Jailor reappears,
approaches, and crosses toward the exit. He unlocks the
door and opens it out again, pauses.

JAILOR

Yes, sir. A long hard way. If I was ever fool enough to commit a killing that would get my neck into a noose, the last thing I would want to see would be a preacher. I'd a heap rather believe there wasn't nothing after death than to risk the station where I was probably going to get off.

> (he waits, holding the door, looking back at them. Temple stands motionless until Stevens touches her arm slightly. Then she moves, stumbles slightly and infinitesimally, so infinitesimally and so quickly recovered that the Jailor has barely time to react to it, though he does so: with quick concern, with that quality about him almost gentle, almost articulate, turning from the door, even leaving it open as he starts quickly toward her)

Here; you set down on the bench; I'll get you a glass of water.

> (to Stevens)

Durn it, Lawyer, why did you have to bring her——

TEMPLE

> (recovered)

I'm all right.

She walks steadily toward the door. The Jailor watches her.

JAILOR

You sure?

TEMPLE
(walking steadily and rapidly toward
him and the door now)

Yes. Sure.

JAILOR
(turning back toward the door)

Okay. I sure don't blame you. Durned if I see
how even a murdering nigger can stand this
smell.

He passes on out the door and exits, invisible though still
holding the door and waiting to lock it.

Temple, followed by Stevens, approaches the door.

JAILOR'S VOICE
(off-stage: surprised)

Howdy, Gowan, here's your wife now.

TEMPLE
(walking)

Anyone to save it. Anyone who wants it. If
there is none, I'm sunk. We all are. Doomed.
Damned.

STEVENS
(walking)

Of course we are. Hasn't He been telling us that
for going on two thousand years?

GOWAN'S VOICE
(off-stage)

Temple.

TEMPLE

Coming.

They exit. The door closes in, clashes, the clash and clang of the key as the Jailor locks it again; the three pairs of footsteps sound and begin to fade in the outer corridor.

(CURTAIN)